The Connecticut Adventure

John W. Ifkovic

GIBBS·SMITH
P
PUBLISHER

SALT LAKE CITY

23 22 21 20 19 18 17 16 15   10   11   12

Copyright © 2002 by Gibbs Smith, Publisher

Published by
Gibbs Smith, Publisher
P.O. Box 667
Layton, Utah 84041

(800) 748-5439
text@gibbs-smith.com
www.gibbssmitheducation.com

Managing editor: Courtney J. Thomas
Associate editors: Susan A. Myers, Anne Robbins, Aimee Larsen
Book design: Richard Elton
Cover photo: Jack McConnell
Other photograph and art credits appear at the end of the book.

Teacher reviewers:
    Barbara E. Mechler   Elaine McLaughlin
    Language Arts Teacher   Teacher
    Hillside Middle School   Western School
    Naugatuck, Connecticut   Naugatuck, Connecticut

Printed and bound in the U.S.A.
ISBN 10: 0-87905-944-3
ISBN 13: 978-0-87905-944-6

Enviro/Tech is a registered trademark.

This book is dedicated to the young people of Connecticut, about to write new chapters of Connecticut history. What you think and what you do are the building blocks of history. Build a history you can be proud of.

Contents

Maps

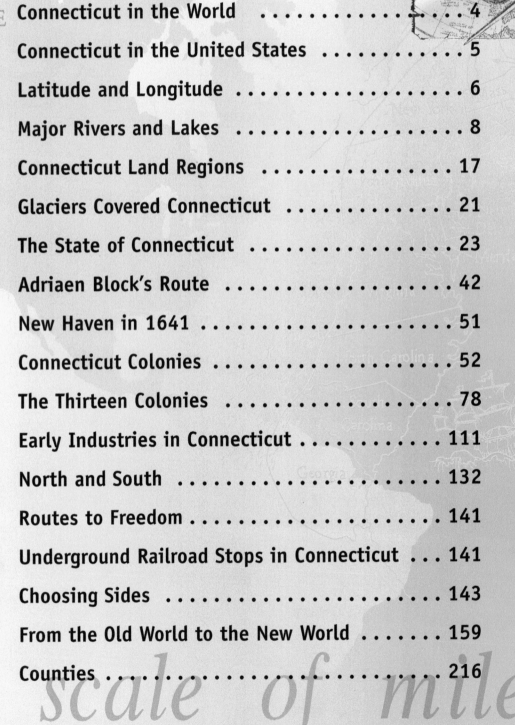

scale of miles

State Flag

State Seal

The state flag and seal both show three grapevines with fruit. The flag's banner has the Latin words *Qui Transtulit Sustinet* on it. Those words mean "he who transplanted still sustains." This refers to the first settlers who moved to Connecticut from Massachusetts. Even though the settlers were "re-planted," they survived and grew, just like the vines.

State Song

Yankee Doodle

Yankee Doodle went to town,
Riding on a pony,
Stuck a feather in his hat,
And called it macaroni.

Chorus
Yankee Doodle keep it up,
Yankee Doodle dandy,
Mind the music and the step,
And with the folks be handy.

Chapter 1

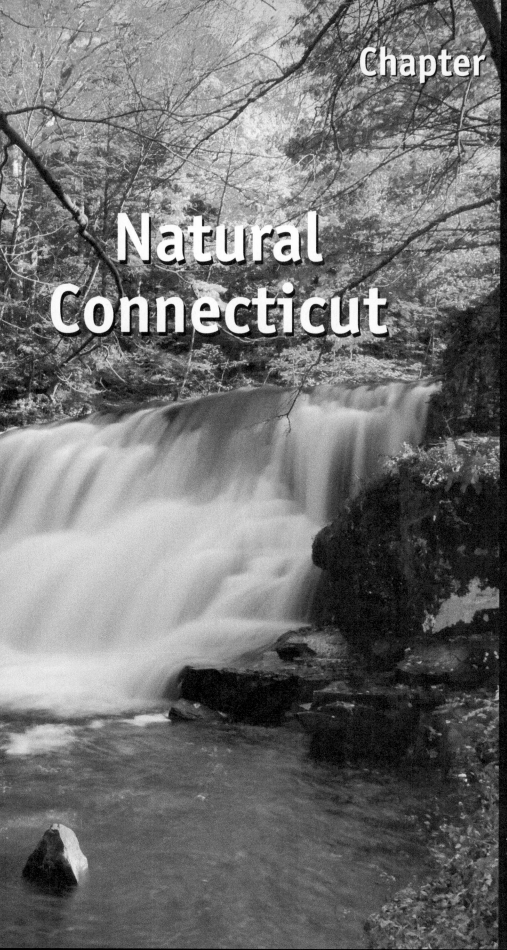

Natural Connecticut

WORDS TO UNDERSTAND

climate
degree
ecosystem
equator
evaporate
extinct
geography
glacier
harbor
humid
latitude
longitude
natural resource
refuge
region
reservoir
sea level
sound
tidal
tributary

Autumn trees burst into color at Wadsworth Falls.

The Land We Call Home

Connecticut may seem large to us. Yet it is just one small part of the world. Because we live in Connecticut, it is important to us. It is our home. Millions of people all over the world live in places that are important to them.

In this chapter we will begin to learn about Connecticut by studying its geography. *Geography* is the study of the land, water, plants, animals, and people in a place. First we will study where Connecticut is located in the world. We will learn what the land is like and how it got that way. We will see how people in Connecticut are connected with people all over the world.

Why is it important to know about the geography of a place? Geography affects where we live and how we live. For example, more people live on flat land than in the mountains. Flat land is easier to farm. It is easier to build houses on flat land. Many people live near the water. They use the rivers for recreation and transportation.

Where in the World Are We?

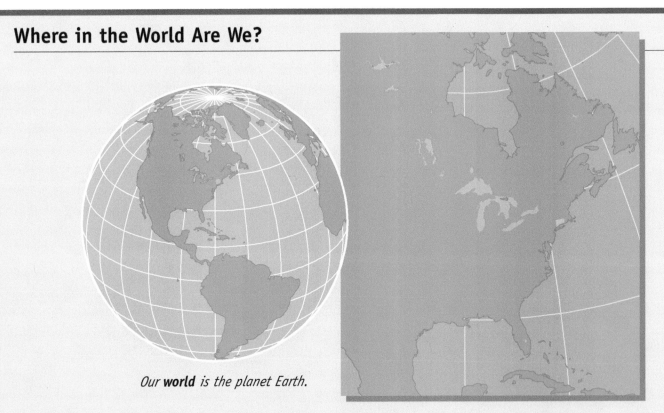

*Our **world** is the planet Earth.*

*Our **continent** is North America.*

The Connecticut Adventure

Location

We all know we live on planet Earth. But just where on Earth do we live? Connecticut is located on one of the world's **continents.** Continents are very large land areas. They have oceans on many sides. Connecticut is on the continent of North America.

Connecticut is part of a **country** on that continent. A country is a region under the control of one government. Our country is the United States of America. Canada is the country to the north of us. Mexico is the country to the south of us.

Our country is divided into **states.** Connecticut is one of fifty states. Connecticut is on the East Coast of the United States. It is near the Atlantic Ocean. Our neighboring states are Rhode Island, Massachusetts, and New York. Can you find all these places on the map?

States are divided into **counties.** Within each county there are cities, towns, neighborhoods, and farms

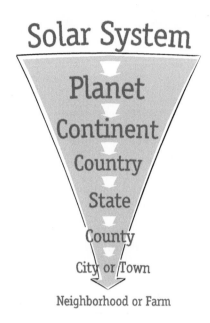

Solar System
Planet
Continent
Country
State
County
City or Town
Neighborhood or Farm

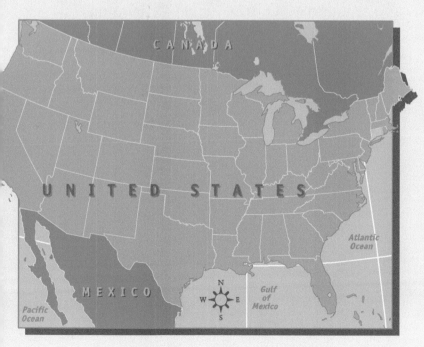

*Our **country** is the United States.*

*Our **state** is Connecticut.*

Lines around the World

Every place in the world has an exact location that is measured by *latitude* and *longitude* lines. You can find these lines on a map or a globe.

Latitude lines run east and west (side to side on the map).

Longitude lines run north and south (up and down on the map).

Along the lines you will find numbers. Each number has a tiny circle by it. This is a *symbol* for a *degree*. A degree is a part of a circle or globe.

The degree numbers all begin at 0. The *equator* is 0 degree latitude. Find the line that is 0 degrees longitude. It is called the *prime meridian.* Find these lines on the globe. The degree numbers get larger as they move farther away from the equator and the prime meridian.

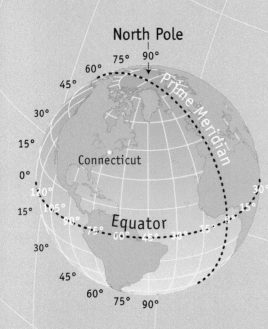

Connecticut is the third smallest state in the country. Which two states are smaller?

Activity

Where Is Connecticut?

Connecticut's main latitude lines are 41–42° North. Our main longitude lines are 72–73° West. You can trace these lines all the way around the world.

1. Which **longitude** line is near the western border of Washington State?
2. Locate about where you live on the map. What is your longitude and latitude?

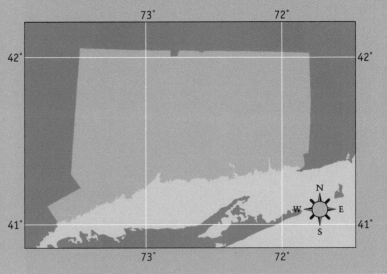

The Connecticut Adventure

Place

What kind of place is Connecticut? Even though Connecticut is small compared to most other states, it has many different features. There are woods and rivers. There are rolling hills and sandy beaches. You can walk along busy city streets or quiet country roads. You can meet many kinds of people.

All places have features that make them different from other places on the earth. Some of these are **natural features**, such as rivers, lakes, forests, soil, and plant and animal life.

Places also have **human features**. There are churches with steeples. There are fences and barns. There are crowded city buildings and lonely lighthouses. These things were made by humans. Roads, shopping malls, and homes are also human features. Both natural and human features make up Connecticut.

"Connecticut. Aren't we lucky? We have wonderful wildflowers, parks, hills, and lovely old houses. We have a pace we like—sometimes slow, sometimes fast. We have rivers, reservoirs, Long Island Sound, a wonderful climate, trees, gardens, snow, rain. And it's a good size—not huge—not small."

—*Katharine Hepburn*

Do you live in the country or in a city? What natural features are around you?
What human features are around you?
(Photos by Scott Barrow)

A Place on the Water

Connecticut borders on Long Island Sound. The Sound leads right into the Atlantic Ocean. Ships can sail from the Atlantic Ocean across Long Island Sound and into our harbors. New Haven, Bridgeport, and New London are our largest harbors. A *harbor* is a sheltered part of a body of water deep enough for anchoring ships.

A Place with Rivers, Lakes, and Ponds

Connecticut has three large rivers. They are the Connecticut, Housatonic, and Thames Rivers. They all flow into Long Island Sound. There are many other small rivers throughout the state.

The Connecticut River is the longest river. Our state was named for it. Long ago, American Indians called the land *Quinnehtukqut*, or "beside the long *tidal* river."

Small canoes and larger boats can both be found at Essex Harbor.
(Photo by Kindra Clineff)

Rivers and oceans are very important for transportation. Which rivers are closest to your home?

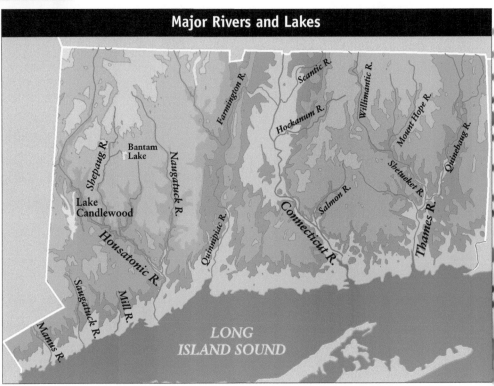

Major Rivers and Lakes

Scantic R.

Farmington R.

Willimantic R.

Hockanum R.

Mount Hope R.

Shepaug R.

Bantam Lake

Naugatuck R.

Quinebaug R.

Shetucket R.

Lake Candlewood

Quinnipiac R.

Salmon R.

Connecticut R.

Thames R.

Housatonic R.

Saugatuck R.

Mill R.

Mianus R.

LONG ISLAND SOUND

The Connecticut Adventure

The Connecticut River was a major trade route for American Indians and early settlers. Today you see mostly small barges carrying oil or gas to Hartford.

Like the Connecticut River, the Housatonic River crosses the entire length of Connecticut. Its main tributary is the Naugatuck River. A *tributary* is a river that flows into a larger river. Find these rivers on the map.

People all through time have used the rivers. The rivers have given them fish, transportation, and waterpower. American Indians paddled canoes along the rivers. The colonists built mills to grind grain beside the waterfalls. People today fish and go boating on the rivers.

How many lakes and ponds do you think Connecticut has? Would you guess 500? 1,000? Keep going! There are about 6,000 lakes and ponds. The largest is Lake Candlewood. It is a *reservoir* made by people to store water for towns and cities. The largest natural lake is Bantam Lake.

Have you ever jumped into a river to cool off?
(Photo by Kindra Clineff)

Growing next to this natural waterfall is our state flower, the mountain laurel.
(Photo by Tom Till)

Keeping Our Water Clean

People eat fish from the rivers and shellfish from the Sound. Fish eat smaller fish. Some small fish eat tiny plants that float in the water.

We must be careful not to pollute the water. Pollution destroys the oxygen that fish and shellfish need to breathe. Polluted water can also block the sun's light. Without sun, underwater plants cannot grow.

All of us can do our part to keep our waterways healthy. What can you do?

Long Island Sound

Have you ever splashed in the water at Long Island Sound? Did you think about the fish that live in the cold rolling water? Did you taste the water? Did you smell the ocean air? What did you hear? What did you feel?

(Photo by Scott Barrow)

At Work or at Play

People work on the Sound. Here are some of the things they do:

- build ships
- fish for oysters, blue crab, flounder, blackfish, bluefish, and mackerel
- trade
- transport goods such as petroleum products, sand, and gravel

People also play on the Sound. They:

- swim
- fish
- boat
- water ski

This Essex fisherman smokes or bakes the bluefish he catches.
(Photo by Kindra Clineff)

Two Kinds of Water

The Sound is a mixture of fresh water and salt water. Where do you think the fresh water comes from? If you said the rivers, you are right! Fresh water from the Connecticut, Housatonic, and Thames Rivers drains into the Sound.

Where does the salt water come from? It washes into the Sound from the Atlantic Ocean. Fresh water and salt water meet when the Connecticut River enters the Sound near Old Saybrook.

Have you seen these special license plates? They were made to raise money to fight pollution. Pollution in the Sound kills fish and shellfish. People are working to keep Long Island Sound clean.

What Is a Sound?

A "sound" is not just something you hear. It is also a narrow strip of water between the mainland and an island. Long Island Sound is between Connecticut and Long Island. See how it works?

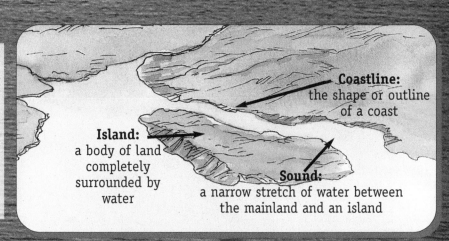

Coastline: the shape or outline of a coast

Island: a body of land completely surrounded by water

Sound: a narrow stretch of water between the mainland and an island

(Drawing by Gary Rasmussen)

It's a Fact!
Long Island Sound is 110 miles long by 20 miles wide. It is about 65 feet deep and has 16 major ports.

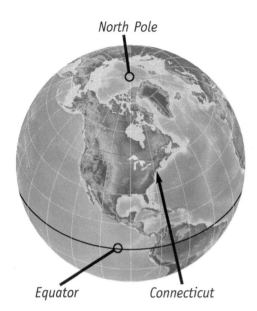

North Pole

Equator   Connecticut

Our Climate

Climate is very important to a place. *Climate* is what the weather is like over a long period of time. The average amount of rain or snow that falls in your yard, the average temperature in summer and winter when you want to play outside, and even the wind blowing in from the ocean all have to do with climate.

Connecticut has long hot summers and cold winters. Why do we have this climate? There are several reasons:

Distance from the equator. The *equator* is an imaginary line around the center of the earth. This is the place where the earth is the "fattest" and closest to the sun.

It is very hot on the equator. Connecticut is not close to the equator, so it is not warm all year long. It is not close to either the North or South Pole, where there is ice all year long. Instead, we have four seasons: winter, spring, summer, and fall.

"Fall means . . . white clapboard churches posed against the fiery reds of nearby sugar maples, the rush of the Housatonic, and the sweet taste of fresh-pressed cider and cider-glazed doughnuts."
—David and Deborah Ritchie
(Photo by Tom Till)

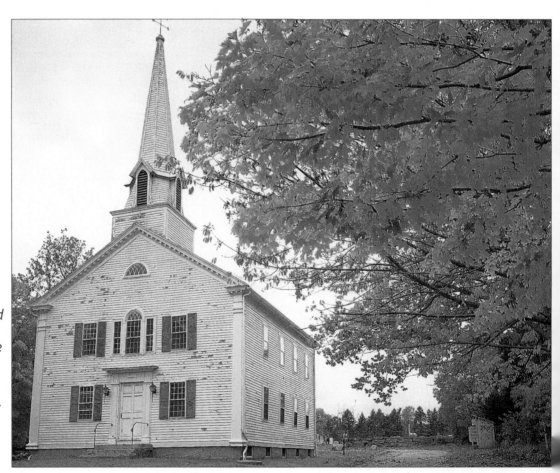

What season is shown here in Bethlehem?
(Photo by Kindra Clineff)

Elevation. Elevation is how high the land is above the level of the ocean. We call the level of the ocean *sea level*. Most of Connecticut has a low elevation, but some mountains in the western part of the state reach over 2,000 feet above sea level. Usually, temperatures are cooler in the mountains than at the seashore. That is why the northwest corner of Connecticut has colder winters than places on the shoreline.

Bodies of Water. Land near an ocean usually gets more rain and snow than other places. The air also holds more water, even when it is sunny. If you hear someone say, "It is so *humid* today," it means there is a lot of moisture in the air.

Where does the moisture come from? Water in the ocean is always *evaporating*. It goes into the air and is carried by wind across the land.

Water affects our climate in another way. Large bodies of water change temperature more slowly than air does. In the winter, the warmer body of water keeps the nearby land warmer. In summer, the cool body of water tends to keep the land cooler. That is why places near oceans usually have milder climates than places in the center of the United States.

Except for the highest mountains, most places in Connecticut get about the same amount of rain and snow each year. Thunderstorms and hailstorms sometimes happen in summer. There have been tornadoes, hurricanes, floods, and ice storms in Connecticut. Fog occurs all over the state. It is most often found along the coast.

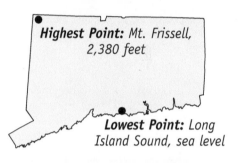

Highest Point: Mt. Frissell, 2,380 feet

Lowest Point: Long Island Sound, sea level

"In the spring I have counted one hundred and thirty-six different kinds of weather . . . inside of four and twenty hours."
—Mark Twain
(Photo by Scott Barrow)

Natural Connecticut

Don't Touch!

If you've ever touched this plant you probably remember the nagging itch you scratched and scratched!

Poison ivy was not common in Connecticut until settlers started clearing the land in the 1600s. When the trees were cleared, the plant had room to spread.

Plants 'O Plenty

Did you know that about half of Connecticut is covered with forests? You can find hemlock and white pine trees throughout the state. There are oak, hickory, cedar, sweet birch, sugar maple, red oak, and butternut trees in Connecticut.

Have you ever wandered through a meadow in springtime? Dogwoods, violets, azaleas, wild cherries, and many other colorful flowers bloom each year. In some places you can pick huckleberries, blueberries, and black raspberries right off the bushes.
(Photo by Kindra Clineff)

Connecticut Critters

Just like plants, animals are a part of Connecticut. At one time, bears were common in the woods and forests. As more people settled here, bears were hunted or forced to move to a new place. Today, you can find animals such as deer, rabbits, weasels, minks, porcupines, skunks, raccoons, and opossums. If you live in a hilly, rocky area you might see a bobcat from time to time.

Are you a bird watcher? Even if you are not, you may have spotted a sea gull, goose, or duck near the shoreline. You may have watched a crow or blue jay circle a meadow. In the winter you may have seen a magnificent bald eagle. These birds and many others make their home in Connecticut.

Have you ever watched a snake slither out of sight as you stepped through the wet grass? Our ponds and rivers are home to many kinds of animals. Connecticut has both fresh and saltwater fish. Trout, perch, bluegill, and salmon like the fresh water in the rivers. Flounder, sea bass, and shellfish such as clams, lobsters, and oysters like the salt water in Long Island Sound.

Have you ever seen a prickly porcupine?
(Photo by Lynn Chamberlain)

Deer live in the mountains and hills.
(Photo by John Lynn)

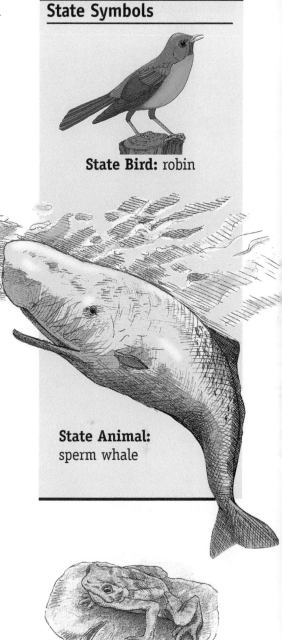

State Bird: robin

State Animal: sperm whale

Have you ever caught a frog at the nearest pond?
(Drawings by Gary Rasmussen)

Connecticut is part of the region known as New England. What other states are part of New England?

Regions

A region is another way to describe where we live. Geographers divide large areas of the world into smaller parts. We call these parts regions. *Regions* are places that have certain things in common. They are alike in some way.

A region can be as large as a continent or as small as your neighborhood. For example, you might live in a coastal region or a mountain region. You probably have a favorite vacation region. You can live in many regions at the same time.

Land Regions

If you were a bird flying high above our state, you would see that there are four different kinds of land. That's a lot for such a small state. We call these land regions. Each land region has mostly one type of landform, such as flat plains or rolling hills.

(Photo by Kindra Clineff)

Western Highland

The land in the Western Highland region is rugged and rocky. There are mountains and hills. The Taconic Mountains are the highest in the state. Some of the peaks rise to more than 2,000 feet above sea level. The highest point in Connecticut is in the Western Highland region. It is Mt. Frissell.

(Photo by Kindra Clineff)

Central Lowland

The Central Lowland is in the middle of the state. The Connecticut River flows through part of this region. There is rich soil in the river valley. People grow apples, our main fruit crop. Hartford, our state capital, is in the Central Lowland region.

The Connecticut Adventure

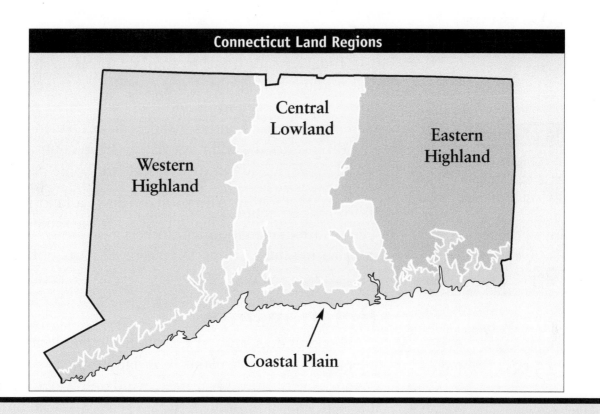

Connecticut Land Regions

Central Lowland

Eastern Highland

Western Highland

Coastal Plain

(Photo by Scott Barrow)

Eastern Highland

The Eastern Highland region has low wooded hills. Granite and other hard, ancient rocks show through the thin soil. Piles of boulders and stones give the Eastern Highland a rocky appearance.

(Photo by Kindra Clineff)

Coastal Plain

The Coastal Plain is a narrow strip of land next to the water. In the summer, people go there to relax, swim, and play in the water. The land has rocky inlets, marshes, and sandy beaches. Our many harbors, such as New London and Mystic, are in the Coastal Plain region. Some of the harbors also have large cities, such as New Haven and Bridgeport.

Movement

Today, people travel from place to place, sharing their ideas and trading their goods. Early people also traveled great distances. They traded ideas and tools with other groups. This made them better hunters, fishermen, craftsmen, and farmers.

People, goods, and information from countries all over the world move in and out of Connecticut. Some people stay for a short time to do business or take a vacation. Others come here to live. When people move, they take their ideas with them. They share information with others. Movement of goods and information links Connecticut with all parts of the world.

Relationships

Geographers study the relationship between the land and people, animals, and plants. Our land is always changing. Some change is very slow. Over time, wind and water wear away rock and soil. However, some natural events, such as hurricanes and floods, happen fast.

People use and change the land. They use the land to meet their needs. They cut down trees. They build cities and roads. They plant new trees. They build bridges, dams, and reservoirs. They dig into the ground to get coal and iron. These things can be important for people. They provide things we all need, including homes and jobs.

If people and industries are not careful, though, they can harm the environment. There was a time when people did not take very good care of the land. They thought there would always be plenty of fresh air and clean water. They didn't think it would matter if they left trash on city streets or sandy beaches. They allowed industries to dump waste into the rivers and the ocean.

Over time, people began to understand how important it is to use the land and water wisely. They passed laws so that factories could not pollute the air and water as much. They set aside some land for state parks and wildlife *refuges*. Today, most people are working together to take care of the land.

A World of Information

In our modern world, the Internet is an example of how ideas and information move. A young girl in Japan can learn all about Connecticut while sitting at her computer. A young boy in Connecticut can learn about Japan while sitting at his computer. They can send information back and forth, or to any part of the world!

It's up to everyone to help conserve natural resources and protect the environment. You can help! You can stop littering. You can recycle cans and paper. You can turn off lights and televisions when you aren't using them. Everyone can help prevent forest fires caused by humans. Everyone can be careful to take care of Connecticut.

*An **ecosystem** is a community. It includes the animals, plants, soil, water, and air in a place. Each part does its own special job to keep the community going. Every living creature is part of an ecosystem.*

Land of Many Natural Resources

Connecticut has *natural resources*. These are things found in nature that people can use. Sand, gravel, and traprock are used to build roads. Plants, animals, and waterways are also natural resources.

The ocean gives us natural resources such as fish and shellfish. A long time ago, American Indians caught these animals for dinner. Today, fishermen catch bluefish, striped bass, lobster, and oysters to sell.

Rivers, streams and waterfalls are a great source of waterpower. In colonial times, people used waterpower to run their mills and factories.

Much of the soil in Connecticut is thin and stony. It is not great for farming. But deeper, richer soils are found in the river valleys. There farmers grow hay, sweet corn, and tobacco. They raise chickens, cattle, sheep, and hogs. They sell eggs from the chickens and milk from the cattle.

These students from Chester Elementary School are learning about the soil.
(Photo by Kindra Clineff)

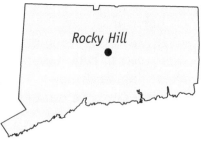

An Ancient Land

Connecticut's land did not always look like it does today. How did it get to be this way? To answer this we must go back millions of years.

Believe it or not, at one time the land we call Connecticut was a place with high mountains. Some of them were volcanoes. They were pushed up by the earth's crust millions of years ago. The mountains rose several times. Then water, wind, and frost wore them down. They became flat plains.

After millions of years of slow change, the land became a hot, wet forest. Dinosaurs and other prehistoric animals lived here. Then the climate changed again. The summers grew cooler. Soon it was cool enough that the snow from winter no longer melted. Slowly it piled up, forming huge sheets of ice called *glaciers*.

The glaciers spread out over much of North America. As the ice got thicker, it covered up the soil and plants growing under it. This time is called the Ice Age.

According to some scientists, it got too cold for the dinosaurs. They disappeared forever.

Dinosaur tracks have been found in Rocky Hill. You can visit Dinosaur State Park to learn about Connecticut's dinosaurs.

Rocky Hill

Ceolophysis

Ceolophysis and Anchisaurus once lived in what is now Connecticut.

Anchisaurus

20

Glaciers Shaped the Land

The weight of the huge ice sheets caused them to move and spread over the land. Sand, gravel, rocks, and boulders stuck in the glaciers. As they moved, they ground down the tops of mountains and widened valleys. Everywhere they went they carried rocks and earth.

Nearly all of the land we call Connecticut was covered by glaciers. The shoreline was much farther out to sea at that time because so much water was frozen in the glaciers.

What happened when the temperature got warmer and the glaciers started melting? Thick layers of boulders, sand, gravel, and clay were left behind. Sometimes the rocks and earth made a natural dam that stopped rivers from flowing over it. This made lakes behind the dams. As the lakes filled with more and more water, they broke through the dams and made a new path to the ocean.

In some places the water just spread out over the land. That land became wet and swampy. When it dried, the land began to look like the Connecticut we know today.

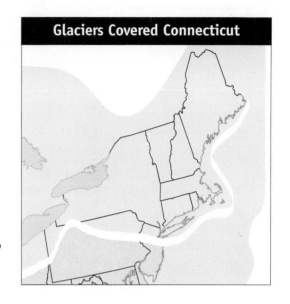

Glaciers Covered Connecticut

*At the end of the Ice Age, very large animals such as mammoths, saber-toothed tigers, and giant sloths lived on the land. These animals are now **extinct**. They no longer live anywhere on the earth.*

Activity

Reading a Map

There are many kinds of maps. Can you think of some? Perhaps you first thought of treasure maps. Or maybe you thought of the road maps your parents use on trips.

Maps help us understand where we are. They help us get where we want to go. It is important to know how to read a map. Most maps have the following features:

Compass

Maps show the directions north, south, east, and west. These are called cardinal directions. In between these directions are northeast, southeast, and so on. You'll find these directions on a symbol called a compass. Most maps have north at the top. A map is much easier to read if you put it so that you and the map are facing north. Then west will be on your left and east will be on your right. Where will south be?

Key or Legend

Map makers use symbols to stand for certain things such as cities, rivers, roads, airports, and campgrounds. Whenever there are symbols, there is a key or legend that explains what the symbols mean. What do the symbols on the right stand for?

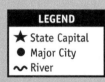

LEGEND
★ State Capital
● Major City
∿ River

Scale of Miles

To show us how far apart things really are, map makers use a scale of miles. One inch on a map might stand for 100 miles on real land. Or one inch might mean 1,000 miles or even more. Look at the map. How many miles are equal to one inch on the scale of miles? Look at a globe and see how many miles one inch stands for.

Chapter 1 Review

1. What is geography?
2. Give an example of exact location.
3. Give an example of relative location.
4. What is the longest river in New England?
5. Name three animals that live in Connecticut.
6. Where is Connecticut's highest point above sea level?
7. Name and describe the four land regions in Connecticut.
8. Why is Long Island Sound important to Connecticut?
9. What other natural resources are found in Connecticut?
10. How did glaciers shape the land?

The Connecticut Adventure

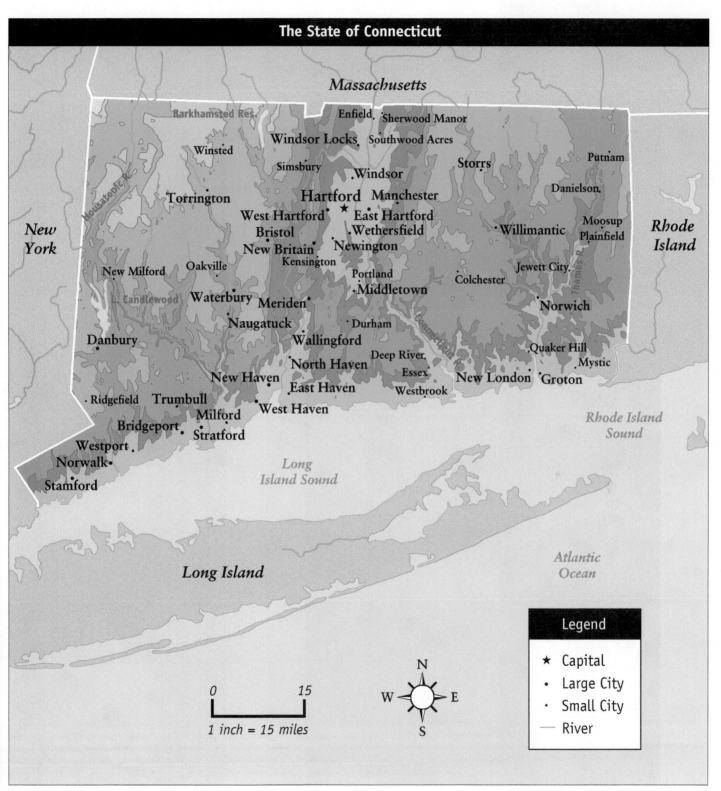

The State of Connecticut

Massachusetts

Barkhamsted Res.
Enfield
Sherwood Manor
Winsted
Windsor Locks
Southwood Acres
Simsbury
Windsor
Storrs
Putnam
Torrington
Hartford
Manchester
Danielson
West Hartford
East Hartford
Moosup
Bristol
Wethersfield
Willimantic
Plainfield
New Britain
Newington
Kensington
Oakville
Jewett City
New Milford
Portland
Colchester
L. Candlewood
Waterbury
Middletown
Norwich
Meriden
Naugatuck
Durham
Danbury
Wallingford
Deep River
Quaker Hill
North Haven
Essex
Mystic
Ridgefield
New Haven
East Haven
Westbrook
New London
Groton
Trumbull
West Haven
Milford
Bridgeport
Stratford
Westport
Norwalk
Stamford

New York

Rhode Island

Housatonic R.

Connecticut R.

Thames R.

Rhode Island Sound

Long Island Sound

Long Island

Atlantic Ocean

Legend	
★	Capital
•	Large City
·	Small City
—	River

0   15
1 inch = 15 miles

N
W E
S

Maps show us location. There are many wonderful places in Connecticut. Do you live near a beach or a river? Which cities are closest to you? How far away from your town is Hartford, our state capital?

Natural Connecticut

Chapter 2

THE TIME
12,000 B.C.–A.D. 1700

PEOPLE TO KNOW
Paleo-Indians
Archaic-Indians
Algonquin Indians

PLACES TO LOCATE
Washington Depot
Hartford
Wethersfield
Windsor
Middletown
Mashantucket
Connecticut River Valley
Massachusetts Bay
Alaska
North America
Asia
Europe

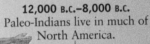

12,000 B.C.–8,000 B.C.
Paleo-Indians live in much of
North America.

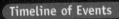 Timeline of Events

12,000 B.C. 10,000 B.C. 8,000 B.C. 6,000

Chapter 2

The First People

WORDS TO UNDERSTAND
archaeologist
artifact
atlatl
council
culture
nourish
pelt
permanent
powwow
sachem
sapling
sinew
tundra
wampum
weir

Paleo-Indians hunted caribou that roamed the Connecticut River Valley.
(Drawing by Marie Litterer, Courtesy of the Pratt Museum at Amherst College)

1,000 B.C.
Algonquin Indians live in what is now Connecticut.

4,000 B.C.   2,000 B.C.   0   1500   1700

8,000 B.C.–1,000 B.C.
Archaic-Indians live in the land we call Connecticut.

1500 ▶ ▶ ▶ ▶ ▶
Europeans begin to explore North America.

Ancient Indians

The first people who came to the land we now call Connecticut were probably following herds of wild animals. They hunted the animals for food. Some scientists believe that people and animals walked across a land bridge that connected Asia with Alaska a very long time ago. Over time, the people spread out over much of North America.

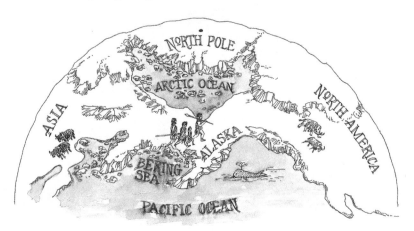

When the glaciers melted, water covered the narrow bridge of land that had connected Asia and North America.

Paleo-Indians

The earliest people were the Paleo-Indians. "Paleo" means ancient. They were hunters who wandered the tundra looking for food. A *tundra* is frozen land without many trees. The people hunted large reindeer, called caribou, and mammoths.

When the people killed an animal, they were careful not to waste any part of it. They ate its meat. They used its thick skin to make clothing and blankets. They even used the bones and sinews to make tools and weapons. *Sinews* are the tendons that connect bones inside an animal.

The Paleo-Indians also fished and gathered wild plants. They lived in small camps near a river or stream, or along the shoreline. When they had used the resources in one area, they moved and set up camp in a new place.

The people learned how to use the roots, stems, flowers, and leaves from plants.

Mammoths were huge animals. The people could get this close only when they had already wounded the mammoth.

(Drawings by Gary Rasmussen)

Archaic-Indians

As the environment changed, so did the lives and tools of the people. The Archaic-Indians came later. They wandered less than the Paleo-Indians. By this time, the land was forested. The people made tools that would help them chop down trees and make canoes. They made an important tool called an *atlatl* (ATL atl), or spear thrower. It let a hunter throw his spear much farther and faster.

The Archaic-Indians hunted bears, deer, and wild turkeys. They fished and caught shellfish. They gathered nuts, berries, and seeds from wild plants.

The people learned to store the food they had gathered in the summer and fall. Then they did not have to move around as much to find food in the winter. They could build more *permanent* homes and stay for many months.

An Archaic hunter used an atlatl to throw his spear farther and faster. Why do you think it was important to keep a long distance between the hunter and a large animal?

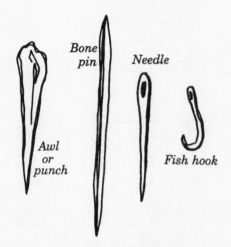

Early people made tools from animal bones.

Awl or punch

Bone pin

Needle

Fish hook

Archaeologists must dig slowly and carefully. They try not to break tiny bones or artifacts that will help them learn about ancient people. Sometimes only a small brush is gentle enough to remove the dirt.
(Photo by David Blanchette)

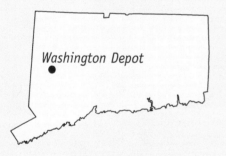

Washington Depot

How Do We Know?

How do we know so much about people who lived so long ago? They did not leave photographs or written records. However, they did leave behind clues about how they lived. The people left artifacts. *Artifacts* are things the people made and left behind, such as spear points, stone tools, trash piles, and graves. Ancient people also left drawings on rocks and in caves.

Scientists called *archaeologists* study these clues to learn about the men, women, and children who lived long ago. Archaeologists have found an early campsite near Washington Depot. Stone knives, spear points, and burned bones have also been found in the Connecticut River Valley.

Algonquin Indians

A long time after the Archaic people lived here, other groups of people came. Because they lived in the eastern woodlands of the United States, we call them Eastern Woodland Indians. The Eastern Woodland Indians who lived in Connecticut were called Algonquins. They shared the same language and lifestyle. They lived in our region for hundreds of years before the first European explorers came.

The most important new idea for the Algonquin Indians was farming. The people still hunted and gathered food, but they began to grow food, too. This meant they could settle down in one place. They no longer had to travel all the time to find enough to eat. However, they did still travel to hunt wild animals.

Many Tribes

Many Algonquin tribes lived in what is now Connecticut. The Pequots were one of the larger tribes. The name "Pequot" means "people of the shallow waters." The Pequots lived in eastern Connecticut, near the Mohegan tribe.

In the winter, Native Americans wore warm fur robes.

The tribes that lived along the banks of the Connecticut River are called River Indians. They lived where the towns of Hartford, Wethersfield, Windsor, and Middletown are today. The Mahicans lived in Western Connecticut.

Dirt trails connected the tribes. Some of the old trails are now modern roads or highways. For example, the Tunxis Trail became the modern road from Hartford to Farmington. The route between the Massachusetts Bay and Hartford is still known as the Old Bay Path.

The different tribes did not have strong ties to each other, even though they had about the same language and *culture*. The strong tribes forced the smaller tribes to show respect to them. Sometimes several tribes joined together to fight an enemy.

Each tribe was led by a chief, or *sachem*. The sachem could be a man or a woman. The sachem made the rules, but he or she always talked with the *council* first. Leading men of the tribe were members of the council.

Life in an Algonquin Village

The people of each tribe lived together in villages. They built villages next to a stream, a river, or Long Island Sound. It was important to live near water so they could cook and wash, catch fish, and travel by canoe to trade with people from other villages.

What do you think?

Why was it easier to travel by water than by land? Is this true today?

What kinds of things do you see around this Pequot home?
How are the people using these things?
(Photo by Allen Phillips, Courtesy of the Mashantucket Pequot Museum)

The Connecticut Adventure

Building a Home

Most Algonquin homes were wigwams. To make a wigwam, people collected young trees called *saplings*. They stripped them of their leaves. Then they bent them into a dome and tied them down. This made the frame.

To make the walls, the people covered the frame with birch bark, mats made of woven grass, or animal skins. They left a hole in the top to let out the smoke from the fire. They left an opening at the front for a door.

Inside, there was a pit lined with stones for the fire. The people built platforms along the walls. They covered the platforms with furs. This made a nice place to rest and sleep.

Sometimes the people built a fence around their village. This was especially important if the chief, or sachem, lived in that village. The fence protected the people if an enemy tribe attacked.

If you were a young girl, you helped your mother tend the fields, care for the younger children, gather wild foods, cook meals, and make clothing from animal skins.

If you were a young boy, you practiced hunting and fishing, helped build wigwams, worked with the women in the garden, and practiced being a good warrior like your father.

Most wigwams were big enough for one family. Larger ones held eight to ten families. What might be growing just outside the fence in this village?
(Drawing by C. Keith Wilbur)

Moving with the Seasons

During the summer months the people lived at the village. They planted crops and watched the cornfields. After the harvest they moved to the forest to hunt. In winter they moved to larger villages in a warmer valley. They needed a place near lots of firewood. In the spring they moved to areas where the fish eggs were hatching. The fish would provide plenty of food.

Moving was easy because the Indians did not have many things. Their homes could be taken apart and rebuilt easily.

Farming the Land

Over time, farming became the most important way of getting food. The most important crops were corn, beans, pumpkins, and other kinds of squash.

Corn was used in many ways. It was a gift from the Great Spirit. It was honored and respected. It *nourished*, or fed, the body and the spirit. Each year the Indians honored corn in the Green Corn Ceremony. It was held just when the corn was ripe enough to eat. The Indians gave thanks to the Great Spirit for giving them corn.

The Indians ate corn fresh from the field or roasted on the fire. They dried corn and ground it into meal. Then they mixed it with meat, fish, vegetables, or fruits. The Indians also made johnny cake. They mixed cornmeal with water and made it into cakes. They cooked the cakes on the fire.

The people did not just throw away the corn husks. They braided them into mats. They used the mats for sleeping or to cover the walls of their wigwam. They used the cobs as scrubbers.

Corn, beans, and squash were often planted together. They were called the "three sisters."

Hunting, Fishing, and Gathering Food

Along with farming, the people hunted, fished, and gathered food. Hunting was best during the fall and winter months. The leaves were gone, so the animals could not hide as well. It was easier to track their footprints in the snow. In the winter, furry animals had their thickest *pelts*.

Most of the time, the hunters caught deer. Deer gave them good meat to feed their families and skin for clothing. Hunters were lucky if they could catch a bear or moose. To catch a large animal, the hunters had to be patient, tracking and stalking it. Then they had to trap the animal.

When larger animals were hard to find, the men and boys caught rabbits, squirrels, and water birds. They hunted them with bows and arrows or nets.

The people used every part of the animal. After eating the meat, they used the skin, feathers, bones, and sinews to make tools and clothing.

To catch a bear, the hunters put a piece of meat under the trap. As the bear grabbed for the meat, heavy rocks and logs crushed the bear.

The people ate fish from fresh water and salt water. They cooked the fish over an open fire. Sometimes the fish were "stone-boiled." The women heated stones over the fire. They put the fish in a container made of tree bark. They filled the container with water, then added the hot stones. This made the water hot enough to cook the fish.

The people also harvested shellfish at the shore. They steamed clams and oysters over the fire.

In the summer there were berries to gather. In the fall there were nuts and roots. The people collected them and stored them for the winter. They dried corn and stored it on woven racks or in baskets. Then they buried it in pits. Dried fruits, vegetables, and fish tasted good in the cold winter months.

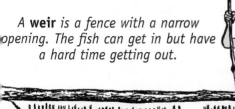

A **weir** is a fence with a narrow opening. The fish can get in but have a hard time getting out.

Making Tools from Nature

How did the people get the tools and other things they needed? They made them out of things they found in nature. They used stone, bone, or wood to make hoes for farming. They used wood and bark to make canoes, snowshoes, and sleds for transportation.

The Indians made axes and knives by chipping stone until it had a sharp edge. They attached the blade to a wooden handle with leather strips or sinews. They made bowls by hollowing out stones or wood. The people carved dishes and spoons out of wood. They wove bags, mats, and baskets from reeds and other plant fibers. They also made pottery from clay and dirt.

There were many ways to catch fish. Can you think of some other ways?
(Drawings by C. Keith Wilbur)

People made the things they needed from what they found in nature.

To make designs on a canoe, the people got the wood wet and scraped a pattern into it.
(Drawings of bowl and canoe by C. Keith Wilbur)

What materials were used to make these snowshoes? Why do you think snowshoes were important?

Making Clothes to Wear

Do you wear a coat in the winter and shorts in the summer? The Indians also wore different clothes at different times of the year. When it was warm, women wore a shirt and a skirt made out of animal skins. In winter they added fur robes. Men wore a kind of apron in summer. In winter they wore leggings and a cape made of skin and feathers.

Women wore their hair loose or braided. Some men did the same. Warriors often shaved their hair except for a strip down the center. They combed bear grease into their hair to make it shine. They also used bear grease on their bodies. It sealed in warmth in the winter and kept away insects in the summer.

For decoration, the people put feathers in their hair. They painted themselves. Often they decorated their clothes with porcupine quills and seashells. They wore bracelets made of stone, bone, and shell on their arms.

Activity

Clothes from Nature
If you had to make your own clothes, using only the things you found in nature, what would you wear? Draw a picture of your outfit. Explain how you made each item.

Giving Gifts

Gifts were an important part of the people's culture. A man who gave a lot of presents was highly respected. When a young woman agreed to marry a young man, the parents gave each other gifts. Gifts were also given to the parents of a newborn child. If a man killed another man, he had to give gifts to the dead man's relatives. Even a good hunter was expected to give away part of the meat from his kill.

The most valuable gift of all was *wampum*. The people made beautiful beads out of tiny shells. They strung the beads together to make patterns. Sometimes the people wore a strand of beads as a necklace. Sometimes they wove many strands into a belt. Symbols or pictures on the belts told important stories.

Why was wampum so valuable? It was very hard to make. It took a lot of work and skill to make holes in tiny shells and string them together.

The people used wampum like we use money. They judged the value of the wampum by how much time it took to make it. But wampum was more than just money. If someone wore wampum while speaking, it was said that he or she spoke the truth. That's why it was often given as a gift of peace.

Can you see the tiny purple and white beads on this wampum belt? Do you think it took a long time to make this?
(Photo by Bob Halloran, Courtesy of the Mashantucket Pequot Museum)

Games and Celebrations

There was a lot of work to do, but the people also played games. Children played with dolls. They dressed them in the costumes of their tribe. The games were fun and they helped sharpen people's hunting and war skills. For example, the Indians practiced their aim with a bow and arrow. They ran races and held contests.

There were dice games and guessing games. The most popular game was lacrosse. It was similar to what we play today, but it was rougher and had fewer rules. There could be up to 200 men on each side.

Linking the past to the present

Are any of the games you play today similar to the ones the Indian people played hundreds of years ago? What games are different? What skills do your games or sports teach you?

A lacrosse stick and ball were used for playing a popular sport.

The Medicine Man

The medicine man was important to the village. The people believed his dreams and visions gave him power. In times of hunger, disease, or danger they called on the medicine man.

Everyone came together in a *powwow*. The medicine man was in charge of the gathering. The people passed around a pipe to smoke. They danced, sang, and said prayers.

Each tribe had a medicine man. He used herbs and plants to cure the sick or wounded.

The Connecticut Adventure

A Spiritual People

Most Algonquin people believed in a Great Spirit. If they lived a good life, they would go to the Great Spirit when they died.

The people also worshiped the animals who gave them food. They believed that the animals were gods who could change their shape into that of a man or woman.

The people made sacrifices to spirits of evil, such as Hobbanock. By doing this, they were asking the evil spirits not to ruin their crops or destroy their hunt.

(Drawings by Gary Rasmussen)

Brave Warriors

Sometimes tribes fought with each other over boundaries o hunting grounds. Sometimes two or three tribes joined together to fight an enemy. War was a test of skill and courage that ever brave warrior had to take. The men held war dances to work u their courage for battle. Then the warriors set out to raid the enemy's villages.

The warriors attacked before daylight, shouting war cries. They used bows and arrows, stone knives, spears, and clubs. Often they made wooden shields for protection. Sometimes the warriors cut a piece of scalp from the victim to show their bravery. Sometimes they took prisoners home with them.

The people made arrowheads out of stones, bones, antlers, eagle claws, and the tails of horseshoe crabs. Sometimes they simply sharpened the wooden tip of the arrow to a point.

Preserving a Way of Life

In the 1600s, Europeans began to settle on the land that ha been the home of the Algonquin Indians. Almost right away, lif changed for Native Americans. We will read about how their lives changed in the next chapter.

There are still Native Americans living in Connecticut toda Members of the Mashantucket Pequot tribe live in Mashantucket. They started a museum to share their history and culture with all people. Many people across Connecticut have some Indian ancestors. Do you?

At the new Mashantucket Pequot Museum you can learn all about Indian life in Connecticut. The museum is owned and run by the tribe.

(Photo by Bob Halloran, Courtesy of the Mashantucket Pequot Museum)

The Connecticut Adventu

Activity

Bury a Time Capsule

Would you like someone in the future to find things you've left behind? What could they learn about your lifestyle?

1. Collect things that describe what your life is like now. Your class picture, a ticket stub from a sporting event or movie, a newspaper, a coin, and an empty box of your favorite cereal are all good things to put in a time capsule. Add pictures you've drawn of things you like (and don't like). You could even make a tape of your favorite songs.

2. Put everything into a waterproof container with a tight lid. Glass and plastic containers work well. Label the container with the date and year you made it. Decorate it for fun.

3. Bury your time capsule in your yard for future people to find.

Chapter 2 Review

1. How did the first people in Connecticut get food?

2. How were the Archaic-Indians different from the Paleo-Indians?

3. Name an Algonquin tribe who lived in what is now Connecticut.

4. A chief was also called a _____.

5. Why did the people build their villages near water?

6. What kind of homes did the Algonquin people build?

7. List three ways the Algonquins got their food.

8. Explain how the people used corn.

9. List three things the people made from what they found in nature.

10. How did the people decorate their bodies?

11. What was wampum? How was it used?

12. What kinds of weapons did the people use in battle?

Geography Tie-In

Give some examples of how the Indian people used the land to meet their needs.

Chapter 3

Timeline of Events

1600

1607 — The first English colony is founded at Jamestown, Virginia.

1610

1614 — Adriaen Block explores the Connecticut River.

1620 — The Pilgrims settle Plymouth Colony.

1620

1624 — The Dutch settle New York and New Jersey.

1630 — Puritans start the Massachusetts Bay Colony.

1630

16 Wethersfield is found

1633 A trading post is started at Windsor Dutch settlers build the House of Good Hope where Hartford is today

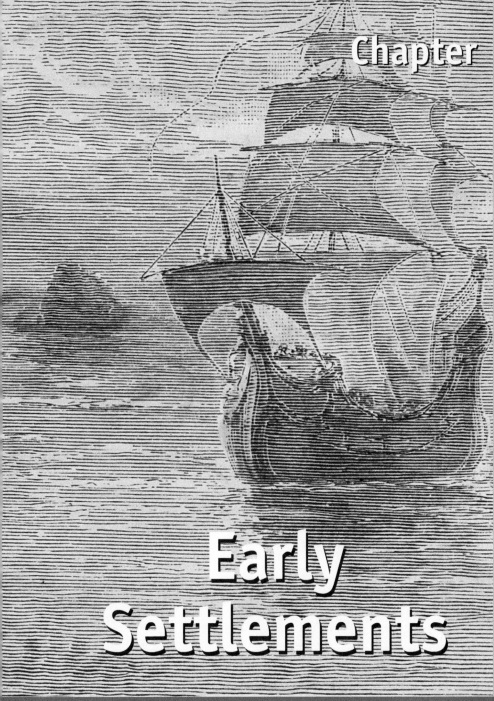

WORDS TO UNDERSTAND
charter
congregation
corrupt
covenant
elect
fertile
grant
influence
massacre
point of view
purify
Puritan
representative
reservation
ritual
town green

Early Settlements

Can you imagine what the first Native American to see a white man must have thought?

36
homas Hooker
unds Hartford.

1639
The Fundamental Orders are written. The three river towns form the Connecticut Colony.

1665
New Haven joins the Connecticut Colony.

1687
Governor Andros rules Connecticut.

1640   1650   1660   1670   1680   1690

1637
The Pequot War

1638
New Haven Colony is started.

1662
John Winthrop Jr. gets a charter for Connecticut.

1675–1676
King Philip's War

1689
Connecticut goes back to government under its charter.

41

Europeans Explore the Land

In the early 1600s, European explorers sailed to the coast of North America. The beautiful land with its "pleasant grasse. and flowers and goodly trees" impressed the explorers. The wrote about a land filled with animals that could be trapped for their fur. The rivers and oceans were filled with fish, they said.

The Dutch

People from Holland were called the Dutch. They set up trading posts and forts in what is now New Jersey and New York. Soon the Dutch began to explore other parts of the East Coast.

In 1614, Captain Adriaen Block explored the Connecticut River. He met some Indian people on his journey. They were friendly to him. They brought him furs from beavers, foxes, and bears. They traded the furs for things such as knives, guns, and cloth.

When Captain Block ran into some rapids on the river, he turned around and followed the river back to Long Island Sound. He found an island that was later named after him.

The House of Good Hope

Sometimes the Indians traded land for the things the Dutch offered. Jacob Van Curler bought some of the land. He and his friends built a small fort there. They named it the House of Good Hope. Today we call the place Hartford.

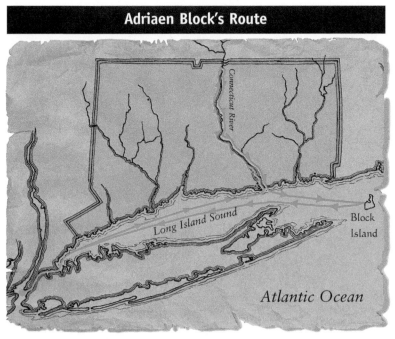

Adriaen Block's Route

Connecticut River

Long Island Sound

Block Island

Atlantic Ocean

Adriaen Block was the first European to explore Connecticut.

Captain Block returned to the Dutch settlement in what is now New York. He made a map of what he had found. He showed other traders the rich furs from the Indians. Soon Dutch traders were sailing into many of Connecticut's waterways, trading with the Indians they met.

The English

The Dutch were not the only Europeans in the region. English settlers had started colonies in Virginia and Massachusetts. Some of the colonists were unhappy with life in Massachusetts. They were thinking of starting their own towns in other places.

The Dutch came to Connecticut mainly to trade. The English came to start towns.

What kinds of things do you see being traded in this picture?
(Drawing by Gary Rasmussen)

The Three River Towns

The first three towns in Connecticut were settled by English colonists from Massachusetts. Windsor, Wethersfield, and Hartford were called the "three river towns."

The Three River Towns

• Windsor
• Hartford
• Wethersfield

Along what river were the three river towns settled?

Windsor

A group of River Indians went to visit the English in what is now Massachusetts. They asked the English to come to Connecticut. They hoped the English could help them get back land they had lost to another tribe. The Indians described the land as beautiful and *fertile*, with many fish and fur-bearing animals.

Edward Winslow left Plymouth Colony in Massachusetts and came to see if the Indians were right. He sailed around the coast and up the Connecticut River. When he got as far as what is now Windsor, he bought land from the Indians.

Winslow wrote a letter to his friends back at Plymouth. He told them about the land. Soon they sent a group of men to do some trading. On their way, the group passed the Dutch House of Good Hope. The Dutch stopped them, but then let them pass unharmed.

When the group reached Windsor, they built a wooden house with a fence around it. They wanted protection from both the Indians and the Dutch.

Sure enough, the Dutch sent men to Windsor to drive the settlers out. But the English were ready to fight back. The Dutch left without firing a shot.

A few years later, more colonists made the journey from Massachusetts to Windsor. The new town began to grow.

Edward Winslow bought land from the Indians and started the town of Windsor.

Wethersfield

Colonists from Massachusetts also settled Wethersfield. Two ministers, Richard Denton and John Sherman, led about thirty families into the Connecticut River Valley. A few of the settlers came directly from England.

Hartford

Thomas Hooker was pastor of his church in Massachusetts. He was a strong Puritan. Even though most of the colonists in Massachusetts were also Puritans, Hooker was not happy there. He and some members of his *congregation* asked for permission to start a new town in the Connecticut River Valley.

Hooker's group listed three reasons for wanting to leave Massachusetts:

- There was not enough land left for cattle.
- The land in Connecticut was rich and fertile.
- They had a strong spiritual feeling that they should move.

June flowers were blooming when Hooker and his group started their journey. For two weeks they followed old Indian trails. Mrs. Hooker, who was ill, had to be carried the entire way on a special bed. When Thomas Hooker and the group reached the end of their journey, they started the town of Hartford.

The three river towns grew quickly. Just a year after Thomas Hooker's group arrived, there were about 800 people living in the towns.

Thomas Hooker led 100 settlers. They brought 160 cattle with them so they could have milk and beef.

Connecticut Portrait

Thomas Hooker
1586–1647

Thomas Hooker was a religious man. He was a *Puritan*. He thought the Church of England should change its ways. Large crowds came to hear him preach in England. The bishops in the Church of England were watching him closely. They warned him to stop his Puritan ways.

Hooker did not feel safe in England. He did not like having to hide what he believed. After moving to Holland, he decided to join the Puritans in New England.

Hooker and his family set sail on the *Griffin* for the Massachusetts Bay Colony. On the ship were several other men who became leaders in New England.

After eight long weeks at sea, the *Griffin* arrived in Boston. The people of Boston were very happy with the new arrivals.

Thomas Hooker and his wife left Massachusetts to start the town of Hartford.

What Is a Puritan?

The people who founded the first towns in Connecticut were Puritans. What is a Puritan? In England, the main church was the Church of England (also called the Anglican Church). Everyone had to worship in Anglican churches. They had to pay taxes to support that church. There was no religious freedom in England or anywhere in Europe at that time.

The Puritans thought that the Church of England had become **corrupt**. They thought things were done for government leaders and not for God. They wanted to change things in the church to make it pure.

There were three main things the Puritans wanted:

1. **Pure Members.** Puritans believed that only people who had been chosen by God to be saved should be members. People should wait until they got a sign from God that they had been chosen.

2. **Pure Worship.** The Church of England had many *rituals* and ceremonies. Churches had stained-glass windows and fancy decorations. There were altars, crosses, and candles. The Puritans believed that churches should be plain.

3. **Pure Organization.** The Church of England had many leaders. The Puritans believed there should be no one higher than the pastor of a congregation.

Puritans were treated badly and sometimes put in prison for their beliefs. That's why they wanted to leave England and start a new life in North America.

The Puritans wanted to *purify* the Church of England. Can you see how they got their name?

The Puritans wanted simple meetinghouses. That way people could think about the sermon or the Bible, not the fancy decorations.

The Connecticut Adventu

Saybrook

Back in England, two men got a *grant*, or gift, of land at the mouth of the Connecticut River. They started a settlement there. They put John Winthrop Jr. in charge. As Winthrop was building a fort for the settlement, the Dutch appeared. When they saw the English flag and cannon, they went away.

Lion Gardiner, an engineer, completed the fort. It was called Fort Saybrook. The town of Saybrook grew up around the fort.

While Fort Saybrook was being built, May Gardiner gave birth to a son, David. He was the first English child born in Connecticut.

The Pequot War

At first, the Indians and the new settlers got along. But more and more settlers started moving to Connecticut. They cut down more trees to make homes. They cleared more fields to plant crops. They scared away many animals. The Indians were losing their land and hunting grounds.

The Pequots were a powerful tribe. They were known as fierce fighters. After Dutch settlers killed the Pequot sachem, the Pequots wanted revenge. They killed an English trader.

After several other Englishmen were killed, Massachusetts sent a group of men to Block Island. They destroyed a Pequot village there and another village near the Thames River. A war between the colonists and Indians had begun.

When the Pequots raided a settlement, they shot arrows and used war clubs like this one. The colonists fought back with guns and knives. Both sides used fire to burn the enemy's villages.

Battles and Massacres

That winter the Pequots attacked Fort Saybrook. They killed nine colonists. In the spring they raided Wethersfield. They killed six men and three women who were working in a field. They took two young girls as prisoners. As the Pequots sailed down the river past Saybrook, they made sure the colonists on the banks could see the girl prisoners.

This made the colonists very angry. An army of men went marching against the Pequots. Captain John Mason led the small army.

The Pequots had been fighting with other tribes over land. They had made lots of enemies. Uncas, the chief of the Mohegan tribe, wanted to join Captain Mason. He wanted to destroy the Pequots.

Mason and his troops went to Fort Saybrook. There they found the captive girls from Wethersfield. The girls told Mason that the Pequots had only sixteen guns and very little gunpowder.

The Narragansett tribe also wanted to help Mason fight the Pequots. On a brilliant moon-lit night, the attackers crept up silently. They surrounded the Pequots' village at Mystic. By the time the alarm was given, it was too late for the Pequots. Mason ordered the village burned. Anyone who tried to escape was chased down and killed.

Most of the Pequots—about 400 warriors, women, old men, and children—died in the flames. Some were taken prisoner. A few escaped. Only two English colonists were killed.

The colonists used guns to fight the Pequots. Only a few Indians had guns at that time.

An hour later, about 300 Pequots came from another village to fight, but their weapons were no match for the English guns.

The Pequots Leave Connecticut

The story of the horrible *massacre* spread quickly among the Indian villages. The remaining Pequots decided to move west along the shore. They hid in a swamp near Fairfield. Still, the colonists decided to go after them. Those Indians who were not killed were taken prisoner. A few who escaped were killed by Mohawk Indians farther west.

From the Pequots' *point of view*, all was lost. They were forced to give up their name and their territory. They were forced to join other tribes, many as slaves.

From the colonists' point of view, there was a new hero— Captain John Mason. They began to feel safe from Indian attacks. Their settlements could grow.

About thirty years after the Pequot War, some land was set aside for them. Some Mashantucket Pequots returned to live together on the *reservation*.

The Connecticut Adventure

The Fundamental Orders

The colonists in the three river towns followed laws and rules made in Massachusetts. After a few years, they wanted to have their own government. Around this time, Thomas Hooker preached a powerful sermon. He said he believed three very important things:

- People should be able to choose their own leaders.
- People should choose wisely, with fear of God.
- People should tell their leaders exactly what duties and powers they could have.

Thomas Hooker's ideas *influenced* many people. The colonists started to write a set of laws, called a constitution. They called it the Fundamental Orders. (That name means the basic rules.) The Fundamental Orders was the first written constitution in the colonies.

Connecticut is called the "Constitution State" because of the Fundamental Orders.

Men from the three river towns met at Hartford to write the Fundamental Orders.
(Drawing by Gary Rasmussen)

Three Towns Become One Colony

The Fundamental Orders was more than just a constitution. It was a *covenant*, or sacred agreement. Whenever Puritans started a new town or church, they signed a covenant.

Under the new laws, the three river towns joined to form one colony. It was called the Connecticut Colony. Later, Saybrook also became part of the Connecticut Colony.

The people in each town chose, or *elected*, people to represent them. The *representatives* formed a General Court. The court met two times a year. It chose a governor and six officials to enforce the laws.

Not everyone in the colony was allowed to vote for the leaders. Women, children, African Americans, and Native Americans could not vote. Only men who were members of the Puritan church could vote.

The New Haven Colony

While the Connecticut Colony was being organized, a second colony was started. It was the New Haven Colony.

New Haven was also started by strict Puritans. John Davenport founded the colony.

Davenport and his wealthy friend, Theophilus Eaton, wanted to have their own settlement. They wanted to start a community built on the teachings of the Bible.

Eaton had heard good reports about the area around the Quinnipiac River. He and others set out to explore the area. Eaton liked it very much. He returned to Boston in the fall but left seven men at the site.

Not long after, Eaton and Davenport returned. They named their settlement New Haven.

The colonists at New Haven agreed to live by the rules of the Bible. They chose religious men to lead them. John Davenport and Theophilus Eaton were among the leaders.

Many of the settlers were wealthy and built big houses. John Davenport's home was built in the shape of a cross. It had thirteen fireplaces. Eaton's house was in the shape of an "E." It had nineteen fireplaces.

On the first Sunday after the Puritans arrived in New Haven, John Davenport preached under an oak tree.

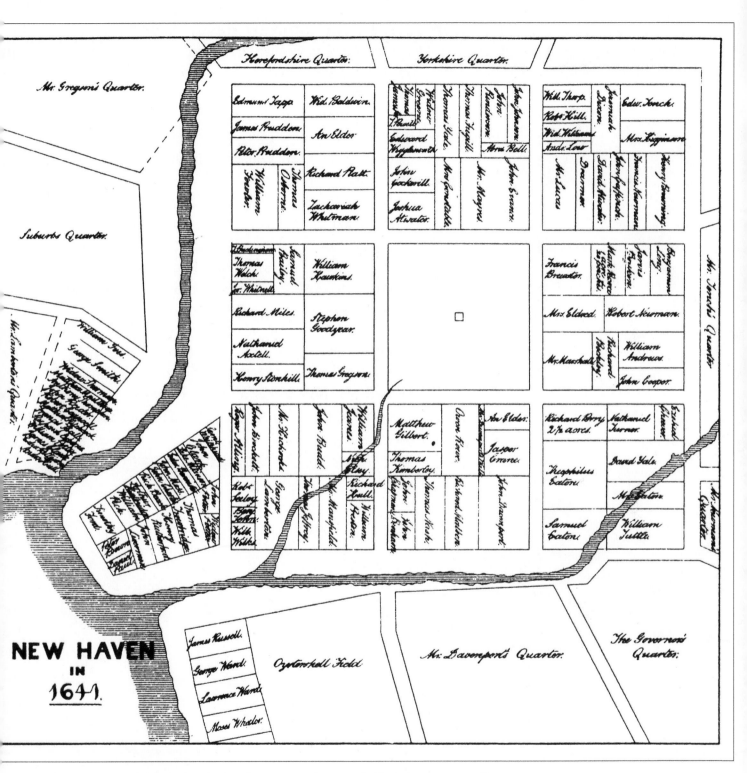

NEW HAVEN IN 1641.

*New Haven was laid out in nine main squares. Streets divided the squares. The center square was a **town green**, where the colonists could meet together. Find the nine squares and the town green.*

Henry Whitfield had some furniture that he bought in England. Most of the colonists did not have such fancy things.
(Photo by Jack McConnell)

New Towns Join the New Haven Colony

The town of New Haven grew. Soon there were other towns along the shore, such as Milford, Guilford, Branford, Stamford, and Southhold (on Long Island).

The towns joined together as the New Haven Colony. They started a government much like the Fundamental Orders of the Connecticut Colony. Only church members could participate in the government.

The Charter of 1662

There was a new king in England who did not like Puritans. What would he do with the Puritan colonies? The colonists worried about losing control of their settlements.

The colonists decided to send Governor John Winthrop Jr. to England to get a charter. A *charter* is permission from the king to settle land. It lets the people set up their own government.

Winthrop was able to get a good charter for Connecticut. It gave the people a great deal of freedom. It said they could vote

Guilford was founded by Henry Whitfield. He built this large house out of stone for his family. It looked like the home of an English country gentleman. It is said to be the oldest stone house in the country.

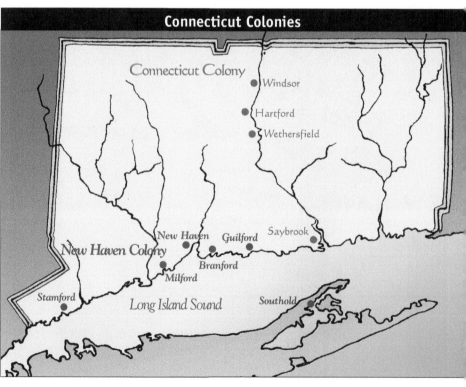

Connecticut Colonies

Connecticut Colony

Windsor

Hartford

Wethersfield

Saybrook

New Haven Guilford

New Haven Colony

Branford

Milford

Stamford

Long Island Sound

Southold

The Connecticut Adventure

or a governor. Every town chose two men to be part of a General Assembly. The General Assembly could make laws.

In the new charter, the New Haven Colony became part of the Connecticut Colony. Now all of Connecticut was one colony.

The charter also stated Connecticut's boundaries. They were different from our state boundaries today. Compare the maps to see how much more land the Charter of 1662 included.

Over the years, Massachusetts, Rhode Island, New York, and Pennsylvania argued with Connecticut about the boundaries. They each wanted part of the land.

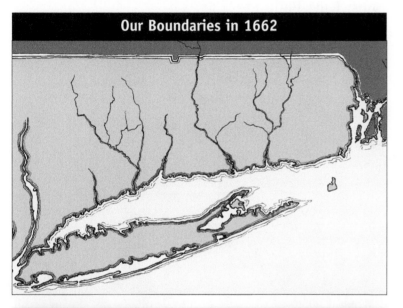
Our Boundaries in 1662

Our Boundaries Today

Connecticut Portrait

John Winthrop Jr.
1606–1676

John Winthrop Jr. was born in England. He studied medicine in Ireland and law in England. After a tour of Europe, he sailed to the Massachusetts Bay Colony, which his father had started.

John Winthrop Jr. helped to start the towns of Saybrook and New London. He served as governor of the Connecticut Colony. He was very popular. Some members of the General Court even tried to change the rule that said how long a governor could serve, just so that Winthrop could continue being their governor.

Winthrop went to England to get Connecticut's new charter. It took him several months, but he did the job well.

King Philip's War

After the Pequot War, the people of Connecticut lived in peace with the Indians for over thirty years. Then they learned that there were problems in Massachusetts.

"King Philip" was the sachem of an Indian tribe in Massachusetts. He wanted to bring all the tribes in the region together to fight the colonists.

Connecticut sent 300 soldiers and 150 Indian men who were friends of the colonists to Massachusetts. They went to fight against King Philip.

Colonists faced King Philip's warriors in the Connecticut River Valley.

The Connecticut Adventu

King Philip's warriors swooped down into the settlements. They burned homes and killed people. Fear spread throughout Connecticut. Everyone worried that the raids would spread to their towns.

The colony's leaders set up night watches in northern Connecticut towns. Patrols guarded workers in the fields and along the woods. King Philip and his warriors did appear in the Farmington River Valley. They burned homes, but no colonists were killed. They had already fled to Windsor for safety.

The colonists fought back. They hunted down King Philip and killed him, bringing the war to an end. The colonists had lost over 600 people. The Indians had lost over 3,000 people, including King Philip. His head was posted on a stake at Plymouth Colony for twenty-five years. After King Philip's War, there were no more Indian wars in the region.

King Philip's real name was Metacom. The English called him King Philip.

The Dominion of New England

When King Charles II died, James became the king of England. He decided it would be easier to rule the New England colonies if they were one large colony.

The king called the large new colony the Dominion of New England. He made Edmund Andros governor.

None of the colonies liked this idea. They wanted to choose their own governors.

The Legend of the Charter Oak

When Edmund Andros came to take control of Connecticut, Governor Robert Treat tried to talk him out of it. He pleaded with Andros not to take their charter. Other men from Connecticut gave long speeches. By the time everyone finished, it was getting dark. The men lit candles and brought out their charter. They unrolled it on the table. Everyone gathered around to see what would happen.

All of a sudden, the candles went out. When they were lit again, the charter was gone!

Edmund Andros

The colonists took Andros prisoner. Why do you think his clothes look fancier than the colonists'?

One story says that a colonist handed the charter through an open window to a man. The man carried the charter to an old oak tree and hid it inside. The tree became known as the Charter Oak.

It made no difference to Andros that the charter had disappeared. Connecticut still had to become part of the Dominion of New England.

The Charter is Restored

As soon as James was no longer the king of England, the colonists arrested Andros and sent him back to England.

The people of Connecticut brought back their charter. They were glad to have their freedom again.

The Charter Oak remained standing in Hartford for almost 200 years. A piece of the tree was blown down during a storm. You can see the piece at the Connecticut Historical Society.

The Connecticut Adventure

Point of View

Sometimes different people see things in different ways. This is called "point of view." Describe King Philip's War from the colonists' point of view. Then describe it from the Native Americans' point of view.

Role Play

In your mind, picture the scene in the legend of the Charter Oak. Write a script of the legend. Let your classmates act it out!

Chapter 3 Review

1. What items did the Indians and early settlers trade with each other?
2. What was the first town in Connecticut?
3. Name one reason Thomas Hooker wanted to leave Massachusetts and come to Connecticut.
4. What did the Puritans think of the Church of England?
5. Why were the Pequot Indians forced to join other tribes?
6. What was the first constitution in the colonies called?
7. Who could vote in the first colonial government?
8. Name the two men who started the New Haven Colony.
9. What is a charter? Why did the people of Connecticut want their own government?
10. Who fought King Philip's War? Who won?

Geography Tie-In

The first towns were settled along rivers. Name the "three river towns." Name the river they were next to. Why did the colonists choose to develop towns along rivers?

Chapter 4

THE TIME
1650–1750

PEOPLE TO KNOW
John Winthrop Jr.
Seth Thomas
Eli Terry
Thomas Hildrup
John Coit
Aaron Cleveland
John Higginson
Eleazar Wheelock
Elihu Yale
Jonathan Edwards

PLACES TO LOCATE
East Haven
Windsor
Farmington
Wethersfield
New Haven
New London
Salisbury
Granby
Hartford
Norwich
Old Lyme
Branford
Guilford
Fairfield
Saybrook
Essex
Middletown
England
West Indies
Africa

Timeline of Events

1650
A new code of laws
tells people how to
live and behave.

1650   1660

1655
John Winthrop Jr. starts an
ironworks in New Haven.

1665
Connecticut becomes
one colony.

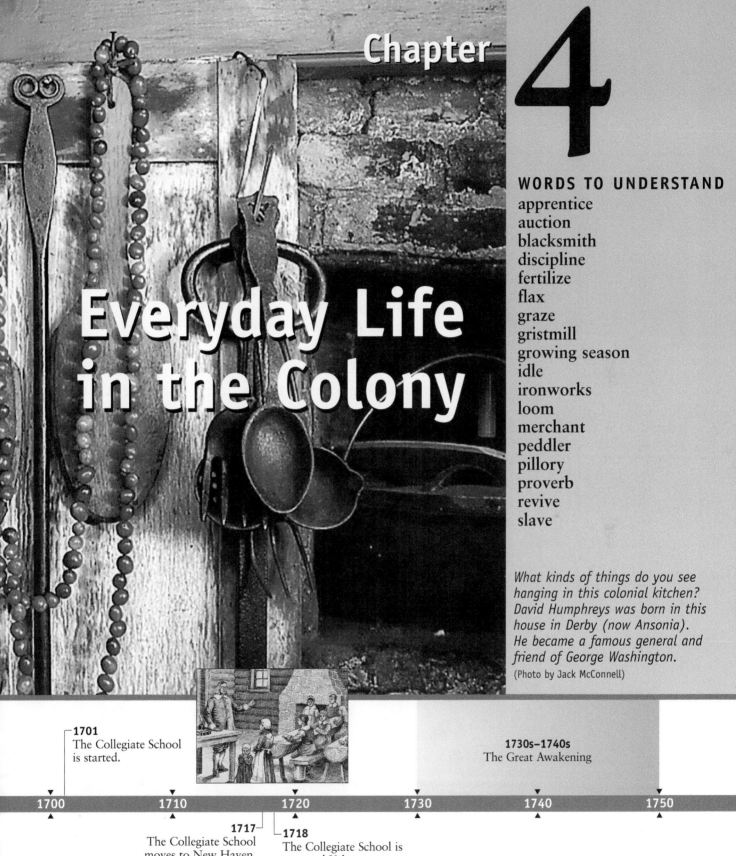

Chapter 4

Everyday Life in the Colony

WORDS TO UNDERSTAND

apprentice
auction
blacksmith
discipline
fertilize
flax
graze
gristmill
growing season
idle
ironworks
loom
merchant
peddler
pillory
proverb
revive
slave

What kinds of things do you see hanging in this colonial kitchen? David Humphreys was born in this house in Derby (now Ansonia). He became a famous general and friend of George Washington.
(Photo by Jack McConnell)

1701
The Collegiate School is started.

1730s–1740s
The Great Awakening

| 1700 | 1710 | 1720 | 1730 | 1740 | 1750 |

1717
The Collegiate School moves to New Haven.

1718
The Collegiate School is renamed Yale.

Life in a Colonial Town

Have you ever visited an old colonial town? Maybe you live in one. Do you ever wonder what life was like for the colonists? Do you ever wonder what they did from day to day?

Most people in colonial Connecticut were Puritans. In fact, the reason they settled in towns was so they could help each other be good Puritans. Religion was very important to them. One of the first things they did was build a meetinghouse, or church, in the center of town.

The Meetinghouse

The people built the meetinghouse near a large grassy area called the the town green. All of the villagers could use this common area. That's why it is also called the town common. Sometimes the people let their horses or sheep *graze* there.

The meetinghouse was more than just a church. People held town meetings and celebrations there. It was a place to come together.

Early colonists put hot coals in this metal box and used it as a foot warmer. On cold days they brought it to church or put it in their carriage.
(Photo by Jean Crossman, Courtesy of the Amherst History Museum)

A family rides to church in East Haven.

Sunday was the day for going to church. The people went to services in the morning. They went home or to the tavern for a cold lunch. (Cooking was not allowed on Sunday.) They returned to church in the afternoon. It was difficult for children to stay quiet and sit still for two long services, but they did.

In some towns, a bell or drum told the people it was time for church. In Windsor, a man blew a horn from the top of the church.

Early meetinghouses were not heated. Sometimes the minister preached with his coat and mittens on! People brought heated stones to keep themselves warm.

Building a Home

The town leaders usually built homes next to the meetinghouse. Most other people were farmers, and they needed room to plant crops. Their homes were scattered around the woods and fields nearby.

The earliest homes in the towns were small. They usually had one room with a chimney at one end. Later, a family might add a second room. Then the chimney would be in the center. As the family and farm grew, a room might be added to the back of the house. This created the "saltbox" style of house.

Neighbors helped each other clear fields and build houses. Trees had to be cut, stripped of their branches, and stacked to make the walls. Then the people added a roof. If the house was going to be made of stone, people had to gather stones and carry them to where the house was being built.

After working all day, the men and women ate together and sang songs or told stories. When they were finished with a house, they built a barn. Then each family planted a vegetable garden.

You can still see many "saltbox" houses around Connecticut.

The Code of 1650

The General Assembly made laws to make sure families were living the right way. For example, if you said a bad word, you had to pay a fine or spend a few hours locked in the pillory. A *pillory* was a wooden frame with holes for a person's head, hands, or feet. If you interrupted the minister, you might have to pay a fine.

Some towns had a jail for people who broke the laws. They also had a whipping post. For punishment, the person was tied to the post and whipped. Everyone could see that he or she had done wrong.

The town leaders took care of the poor and kept an eye out for strangers.

This bronze bowl was used to measure grain.

Inside the house, everyone gathered around the large kitchen fireplace.
This woman shows how colonial women cooked over the fire.
In the evening, men read by its light. Everyone enjoyed its heat.
(Photo by Kindra Clineff)

Linking the past to the present

Why do you see so many rock walls around New England? Long ago, farmers built the walls by hand as they cleared their land of heavy rocks and stones. They stacked them up to form fences around their fields.

Taverns and Inns

Near the center of town was a school-house, a **blacksmith's** shop, and a general store. At the general store the people bought coffee, sugar, and spices. Most of the other things they made or grew themselves.

As old Indian trails became dirt roads, taverns and inns opened along the routes. Most taverns had bedrooms where travelers could rest and eat a nice meal. But taverns were also important to the townspeople. They had large rooms for meetings, dances, and even elections.

People went to the tavern to eat, relax, meet neighbors, gossip, and talk about politics.

Marriage and Family Life

The colonists celebrated births and weddings, just like we do today. Eight days before a young couple got engaged, they had to make a special announcement in the town. Eight days before the wedding, they had to make another announcement. Connecticut was the only colony that had this rule.

The father was the head of the family. He was held responsible for the behavior of his wife, children, and servants. Everyone had to listen to him and obey him. No father wanted to be punished for something his children did wrong. When a woman married, her place, it was said, was "to guide the house and not guide the husband."

Families were large, with seven or eight children. Children were very important because they helped with the work on the farm and in the home.

Find the bride and groom at this Puritan wedding.

Time to Work

Pretend you are a child in a colonial town. At dawn, your mother comes to wake you up. You beg to stay in your warm bed, but you know there is work to do. You put on your clothes and race your sister to the kitchen for breakfast.

You are glad to see a jug of fresh warm milk on the wooden table. That means your older brother has already milked the cow and fed the horses. You stand by the warm fire while your mother makes johnnycake and mush for breakfast.

You've been doing chores since before you were seven. Your father always says that *idle* hands are sinful. What will he ask you to do today?

A Young Girl's Work

Pretend you are a young colonial girl. You help your mother cook and serve the food. You clean the house from top to bottom. You help take care of the younger children. You spin the thread to make cloth and help sew the family's clothes. When the clothes are dirty, you take them outside and wash them. You even make the soap. You help in the garden. You learn these things so you can take care of your own house and family one day.

To make work more fun, children turned their chores into games. They had contests to see who could carry the most wood. They sang songs to pass the time.

Soap was made from fireplace ashes and animal fat. It was not soft, and it didn't smell as nice as soap does today, but it got the clothes clean.

The Connecticut Adventure

A Young Boy's Work

Pretend you are a young colonial boy. You chop wood and bring it in for the fire. You feed the chickens and horses and clean the barn. In the garden, you pick berries, pull weeds, and gather vegetables. Sometimes you run errands for your parents.

By the time you are ten or twelve, you have to think about what you will do for a living. You can do what your father does or learn a new trade. Maybe you will decide to go to college and become a minister.

What do you think?

If you had to decide right now what to do for a living, what would you choose?

Spinning and Weaving

Women and girls used a spinning wheel to turn a plant fiber called *flax* into thread. They spun sheep's wool into yarn.

Once the women had made thread, they used a *loom* to weave the thread or wool into cloth. They cut the cloth and sewed clothes to fit each family member.

(Photo by Jack McConnell)

Time to Play

Even though there was much work to be done, children still had time to play. In the summer they went swimming in a pond or river. They flew kites and played games outside. Some of the favorite games were leapfrog, hopscotch, horseshoes, and hop-skip-and-jump. Do you play any of those games in the summer?

In winter the family often climbed in the wagon, bundled up in blankets, and set out across the fields on a sleigh ride. It was fun to hear the jingle of the sleigh bells as the horses trotted along. Back home by the fire, children played with cornhusk dolls or made paper hats.

What Did They Wear?

Farmers and Craftsmen

Colonial farmers needed clothes that were comfortable to work in all day. They wore simple pants and coats. They wore stockings and leather shoes.

Women wore linen dresses and sometimes tied a shawl around their necks. Their skirts were not too long because they would get dirty. Young children wore the clothes their brothers and sisters had outgrown. In the summer they went barefoot.

Merchants

Merchants in the seaports wore fancier clothes. They could afford to hire a tailor to make their clothes for them. The town of Farmington had a tailor as early as 1697. Men wore velvet and satin from England. They wore shirts with frills, shoes with shiny buckles, and hats. White wigs were very popular, too. Wealthy women wore fancy dresses with hoops, bows, and lace.

Girls try to catch a chicken on a colonial farm.

Earning a Living

Farming

Most colonists in Connecticut were farmers. The soil was not very good for growing crops in some parts of the colony, but the river valleys had moist, rich soil. Along the shore, the *growing season* was long. This means there was a long time between the last frost of spring and the first frost of fall.

Thanks to the Native Americans, the colonists knew how to grow corn. Farmers planted it like the Indians did, on small hills a few feet apart. They used fish to *fertilize* the soil.

Farmers also grew beans, pumpkins, peas, rye, wheat, flax, hemp, barley, and oats. People in Wethersfield grew lots of onions. People in Windsor grew tobacco plants. Apple and pear trees and berry bushes grew well. The colonists made apple cider and brandy from the fruit.

Some farmers raised animals. They kept sheep for their wool. They raised pigs and cattle for their meat. They grew grasses such as red clover and timothy to feed the cattle. Over time, the farmers began to raise more cattle, hogs, and horses than they needed. They shipped them across the ocean for sale.

Sometimes bugs or birds got into the corn fields. An old farmer's rhyme tells of the problems with growing corn:

One for the bug,
One for the crow,
One to rot,
And two to grow.

According to the rhyme, how many seeds of corn did a farmer need to plant?

Crafts and Trades

Some people did not farm for a living. They made things and sold them to other people. They made shoes, hats, or furniture. Every town also needed a blacksmith to make iron goods, such as horseshoes. John Winthrop Jr. started the first *ironworks.* Men made nails, kettles, and other goods out of iron.

Craftsmen always needed helpers. Some young men found work as apprentices. An *apprentice* was a person who lived with a craft worker and learned the trade. The craftsman gave the apprentice food, clothes, and a place to live.

Most towns had a *gristmill* where a miller ground grain into flour. Workers at sawmills cut logs into neat pieces of wood for building. A whole tree trunk could be cut at the sawmill. It was much faster than chopping with an ax.

Making clocks was an important trade in Connecticut. In later years, people from all over New England wanted the beautiful clocks made by Seth Thomas and Eli Terry. Watches and brass items were also made in Connecticut.

Other colonists worked with natural resources. They found iron ore in New Haven, New London, and Salisbury. They used copper found in Salisbury and Granby.

This tall case clock was made by Thomas Hildrup of Hartford.

Jobs in Colonial Connecticut

apothecary [pharmacist]
baker
blacksmith
bookkeeper
brazier [works with brass]
brewer
candle maker
carpenter
cooper [makes barrels and tubs]
doctor

glazier [works with glass]
gunsmith [makes guns]
miller [runs a mill to grind flour or make paper]
needle maker
portrait painter
silversmith [works with silver]
stonemason [works with stone]
tanner [works with leather]
teacher
wheelwright [makes wheels]

1. Are all of these jobs still around today?
2. Why do you think some of the jobs are no longer needed?
3. What job would you have liked to do?

The Connecticut Adventure

THE WATERWHEEL

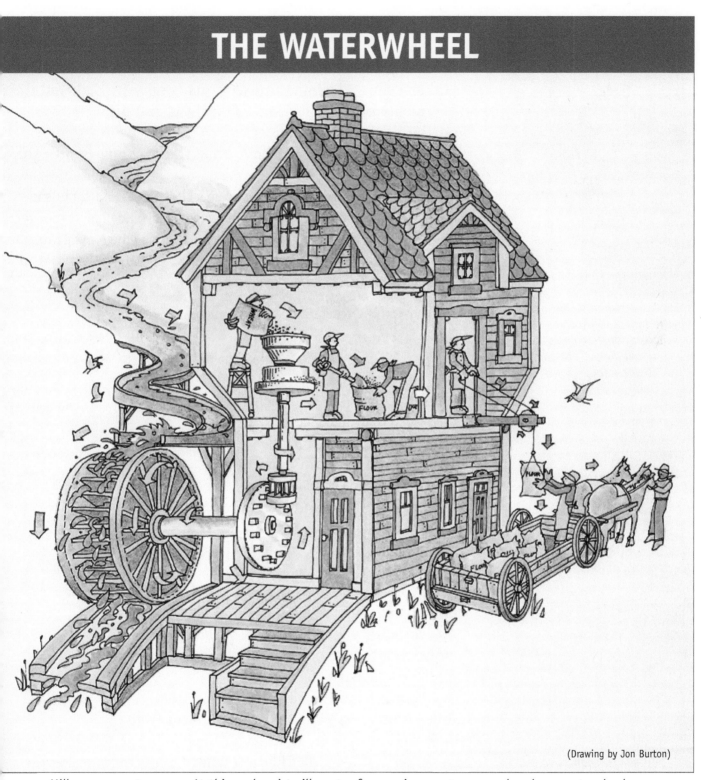

(Drawing by Jon Burton)

Mills ran on waterpower. At this early gristmill, water from a river or stream made a large waterwheel go around and around. As the waterwheel turned, it moved levers that turned a millstone. As the millstone turned, it ground wheat into flour. The flour was then put into bags and sold.

Shipbuilding

Shipbuilding became important along the rivers and the shore of Long Island Sound. These were perfect places for building ships. Sailing ships were made out of wood, and there was plenty of wood nearby. There was also plenty of water nearby, so the ships did not have to be moved across land.

At first, the colonists built small trading ships. Later, they built larger ships.

John Coit started New London's first shipbuilding business in the 1660s. New London was an important place for shipbuilding. Shipbuilding was also good business in Norwich, New Haven, Old Lyme, Branford, Guilford, Fairfield, Saybrook, Essex, and Middletown.

Ship carvers had workshops near the ports. They carved fancy decorations for large ships and simple designs for smaller boats.

Trading Goods

Merchants opened country stores. The people went to the stores for spices, sugar, molasses, rum, many kinds of cloth, gunpowder, and glass.

Merchants stocked their shelves by trading their seeds, grain, cheese, lard, horses, cattle, vegetables, apples, and cider to other merchants near the shipping ports. Those merchants went to trade in larger ports such as Boston, Providence, Newport, or New York. Goods from Europe and the West Indies came into these large ports.

People in the West Indies wanted the flour, pork, and codfish the colonists had. The colonists wanted the rum, sugar, and molasses the West Indians had. Both groups traded to get what they wanted.

People from New England were often called "Yankees." Yankee *peddlers* went from door to door selling goods to farmers. Some people were excited to see what the peddler had brought. Others did not like the peddlers because they thought they charged too much money.

At the printing press, men printed newspapers to sell.

Peddlers w[...] from town [...] town, sel[...] their goo[...]

What Did They Trade?

Have you ever made a good trade with a friend? What did you give? What did you get? Look at the chart to see what the colonies had to trade and what they wanted in return.

Colonies	West Indies
beef	rum
barrels	molasses
boards	sugar
cheese	coffee
flour	spices
fruits & vegetables	

The Slave Trade

Some people came to the colony as *slaves*. Slaves were taken from their homes and forced to work in a new place. Most slaves were black people from Africa. They were brought to America on crowded ships. Other slaves were Indians who had been taken as prisoners.

Slaves had to work on farms or in homes. They did not get paid. They were not free to live their own lives. Although they were people, they were sold like goods or animals.

Many people made money trading slaves. Some sea captains from Connecticut were slave traders. They bought and sold slaves at auctions. An *auction* is a sale where whoever bids the highest gets to buy the goods.

Compared to the other colonies, Connecticut did not have many slaves. Some people owned one or two slaves. They often cared for and protected them like members of the family. They taught them to be Christian, and sometimes to read and write.

Slaves were kidnapped from their homes in Africa, chained together, and forced onto ships that took them far away.

At this time, only a few Connecticut citizens thought slavery was wrong. Aaron Cleveland, a minister in Norwich, may have been the first to write about how wrong it was to make people slaves. We will read more about slavery in a later chapter.

Free African Americans

Not all black people in the colony were slaves. Free African Americans worked as farmers or paid servants. Some worked at the shipyards along the coast.

Free African Americans had the right to go to church, celebrate holidays, and get married. Some were able to buy land and start their own businesses. However, blacks had to carry passes when they went from town to town. They were not allowed to argue or fight with whites. They did not enjoy the freedoms that other colonists enjoyed.

Colonial Schools

Education was very important in colonial Connecticut. People had to be able to read and write so they could learn the Bible and the laws of the colony. The law said that each week parents had to teach their children to read English.

When a town had at least fifty families, it had to have a teacher of reading and writing. When there were 100 families, the town had to set up a school to prepare its boys for college.

In Hartford, Reverend John Higginson set up Connecticut's first school. Soon, free schools began to open around the colony.

Most schoolbooks had religious lessons in them. One example was *The New England Primer*. Children learned the alphabet by learning a rhyme for each letter. For "A" the student said, "In Adam's fall, we sinned All." For "F" it was "The Idle Fool is whipped at school."

Look around at your classroom. Now look at this colonial classroom. What is different? Is anything the same?

The grammar books also taught Latin and Greek to prepare students for college.

Reverend Eleazar Wheelock started a school for Native Americans. He opened a second school to train Indians to be missionaries. Then they could go out and teach other Indians about Christianity. Years later, the school moved to New Hampshire and became Dartmouth College.

Connecticut's First College

At first, the only college in New England was Harvard in Massachusetts. The people of Connecticut wanted their own college so they did not have to send the boys so far away. It cost a lot of money to send boys all the way to Harvard.

A group of ministers asked the General Assembly to set up a college. They started a college in Saybrook, then moved it to New Haven. At first it was called the Collegiate School. The name was changed to Yale College after a wealthy man named Elihu Yale gave money to the school.

Can you imagine going to college in just a few years? Boys started studying at Yale when they were fourteen or fifteen. They graduated before they were twenty. There were no colleges for girls in colonial times.

A hornbook was a wooden board with letters and sentences written on it. Children learned to read from hornbooks. Can you read this hornbook?

Yale College (now called Yale University) became one of the best colleges in the country.

New Haven

A Typical Day at Yale

In the early days at Yale, all of the students got up at six o'clock in the morning. They began the day with prayers. Then they went to classes all morning. They ate a mid-day dinner, then went to more classes. After supper the students were free until nine o'clock. They studied until the lights were turned out at eleven.

Students learned Latin, Greek, Hebrew, physics, math, and other difficult subjects. Life at Yale was strict, but some students found ways to have fun. For example, they stole hens and other animals as pranks or played cards.

Linking the past to the present

The first colleges taught boys to become ministers. Soon they taught other subjects, such as science. Girls did not go to college. Today, whether you are a boy or a girl, you can study almost any subject at college.

The Great Awakening

As time passed and towns grew, it was harder to keep *discipline* in the church. People were not living by the strict rules anymore. Newcomers with different religions were settling in Connecticut. More and more Quakers and Baptists were moving in. The Puritan church leaders did not like this.

Puritan preachers tried to get the colonists to wake up, or *revive* their religious feelings. They held meetings called revivals. At the meetings they gave powerful sermons, throwing their hands in the air and shouting. Jonathan Edwards scolded the colonists for being too relaxed about religion. He told the sinners what would happen if they did not change:

> . . . imagine yourself being cast into a fiery oven, . . . where your pain would be . . . greater than . . . touching a coal fire. . . . Imagine also that your body were to lie there for a quarter of an hour, full of fire, . . . what horror would you feel . . . But what . . . if you knew you must lie there . . . a whole year; . . . O then, how would your heart sink, . . . if you knew, that you . . . must bear it forever and ever!

During the sermons people cried, fainted, or danced around. They claimed to have visions. Religious revivals swept through the

Jonathan Edwards' powerful sermons started the Great Awakening.

The Connecticut Adventure

colonies. Many people who had not been very religious joined churches or started new ones. We call this the Great Awakening.

Activity

Critical Writing

There is a Danish *proverb* that says, "Children are the poor man's wealth." Go through the chapter and review the role of children in colonial times. How did they help the adults at home? On the farm?

Write a few paragraphs about how this proverb applies to life in colonial Connecticut. Make sure to include examples from the textbook. You could even illustrate your writing with a drawing of a colonial child at work.

Chapter 4 Review

1. Why did the colonists build meetinghouses in the center of their towns?
2. Name two ways people were punished in colonial times.
3. What were taverns used for?
4. What kind of work did the women and girls do?
5. What kind of work did the men and boys do?
6. What was the most popular job in colonial Connecticut?
7. What is an apprentice?
8. Name some items the colonists traded with people in the West Indies.
9. What is a slave auction?
10. How was religion taught in the schools?
11. Why did the people of Connecticut want their own college?
12. How did the Great Awakening change religious life in the colonies?

Geography Tie-In

1. How did Connecticut's location affect trade in colonial times?
2. Why was Connecticut's location important to the shipbuilding industry?
3. Why was the length of the growing season important to colonial farmers?

THE TIME
1750–1800

PEOPLE TO KNOW
George Washington
Jared Ingersoll
Israel Putnam
Paul Revere
Thomas Jefferson
Hannah Bunce Watson
Samuel Huntington
Roger Sherman
William Williams
Oliver Wolcott
Jonathan Trumbull
Nathan Hale
Benedict Arnold
Nero Hawley

PLACES TO LOCATE
Danbury
Ridgefield
Greenwich
New Haven
Fairfield
Norwalk
New London
Groton
Thirteen Colonies
Boston, Massachusetts
Lexington, Massachusetts
Concord, Massachusetts
Philadelphia, Pennsylvania
Chesapeake Bay
England
France
Canada

The Struggle for Independence

Timeline of Events

1750

1755
The Connecticut Gazette is the first newspaper in the colonies.

1754–1763
French and Indian War

1760

1765

1765
The Stamp Act is passed.

1764
The Sugar Act is passed.

1767
The Townshend Acts are passed.

1770
Boston Massacre

WORDS TO UNDERSTAND

ammunition
astronomy
boycott
customs house
delegate
empire
fleet
frontier
independence
loyalist
militia
patriot
privateer
protest
provision
revolution
tax
traitor

Colonial men left their wives and children to fight for liberty.

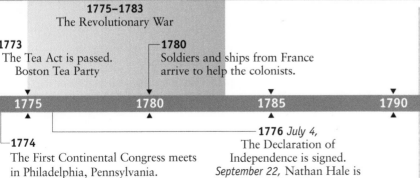

1775–1783
The Revolutionary War

1773
The Tea Act is passed.
Boston Tea Party

1780
Soldiers and ships from France
arrive to help the colonists.

1775   1780   1785   1790   1795   1800

1774
The First Continental Congress meets
in Philadelphia, Pennsylvania.

1776 *July 4,*
The Declaration of
Independence is signed.
September 22, Nathan Hale is
hanged for treason.

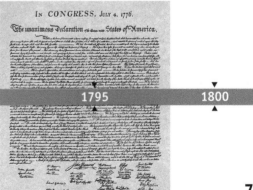

Early Signs of Trouble

Connecticut's charter gave the people a great deal of *independence*. They could choose their own leaders and make many of their own laws. But Connecticut was still part of the British *Empire*, or kingdom. It was still a colony that belonged to England.

England is part of Great Britain. That's why English people are also called British.

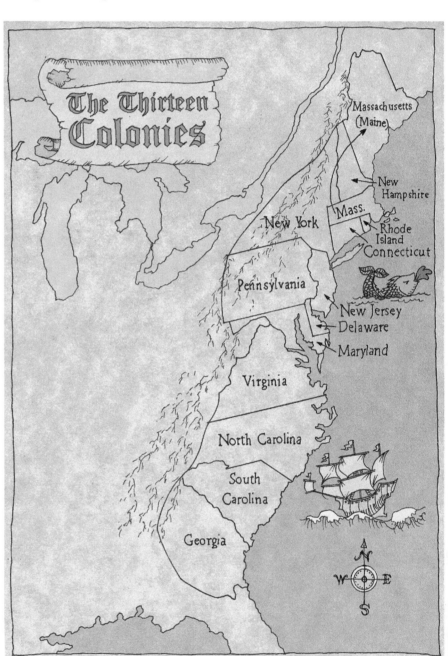

The Thirteen Colonies

Massachusetts (Maine)

New Hampshire

Mass.

New York

Rhode Island

Connecticut

Pennsylvania

New Jersey

Delaware

Maryland

Virginia

North Carolina

South Carolina

Georgia

N W E S

By the mid-1700s, England had thirteen colonies in North America.

Fighting for the Frontier

England had thirteen colonies in North America, but France controlled the land around the colonies. Both England and France wanted their empires to grow. They went to war to get more land.

The Indians who lived around the colonies and in Canada also wanted the land. It had been their home for a very long time. Because they still wanted to trade furs with the French, they helped the French fight the British.

England got men from its colonies to help in the fight against France. Connecticut sent soldiers, guns, and supplies to the *frontier*. The colonists called this the French and Indian War because they were fighting against the French and the Indians.

Important Results for America

After many years, England won the war. It won control of land all the way to the Mississippi River and in Canada. American men had gained military experience. They had practiced fighting in colonial *militias*, or armies. Men like George Washington had learned to command troops. These things were important for what was about to happen.

The frontier is the edge of settled land where it becomes wilderness.

Trouble Brews

The French and Indian War had cost a lot of money. The British wanted the colonists to help pay for the war.

The colonists believed that they had already paid. They had given men and supplies. But England decided to *tax* the colonists to raise money. They made new laws that made the colonists very angry.

The Sugar Act

England passed the Sugar Act, which put a tax on sugar and molasses sold in the colonies. The British tried to force the colonists to buy sugar from islands claimed by the British, instead of from other islands.

Merchants in the colonies wanted to decide for themselves who they would trade with. They also thought it was unfair to make them pay taxes.

The Stamp Act

Next the Stamp Act was passed. It said the colonists had to use special paper for marriage licenses, wills, newspapers, and even playing cards. The special paper had a government stamp on it. It cost the colonists money. Everyone used these things, so everyone had to pay.

"No Taxation without Representation!"

What made the colonists so mad was that they were not allowed to send representatives to vote in Parliament. (Parliament is the law-making group in England.) Because of this, they thought Parliament should not be allowed to tax them.

The colonists argued with the British over the Stamp Act.

People all across Connecticut *protested*. They wrote letters to the General Assembly, saying how unfair the taxes were. A special group helped the governor prepare a letter to send to England. It said there must be "no taxation without representation."

People in Connecticut Take Sides

People in western Connecticut thought they should just accept the stamp tax, even though they didn't like it.

People in eastern Connecticut were bursting with anger. They did not want to pay the tax. Some joined a secret group called the Sons of Liberty. The Sons of Liberty began to protest the taxes.

Jared Ingersoll of Milford took the job as tax collector. One day, he was on his way to Hartford for a meeting. About 500 Sons of Liberty met him in Wethersfield. They were carrying clubs and wearing militia uniforms. They forced him to say he would give up his job as tax collector. Then they followed him to Hartford and made him say it again in front of the General Assembly.

The Townshend Acts

England took away the Stamp Act, but it passed another set of taxes. The Townshend Acts taxed British tea, glass, paper, paint, and other things people needed.

Again the colonists sent a protest letter to England. They said the taxes went against Connecticut's charter. Only Connecticut should tax itself. Again, they said there should be "no taxation without representation!"

The colonists stopped buying the things from England and paying the tax. They tried to get everyone to *boycott* the British goods. By 1770, only one of the taxes remained—the tea tax.

Words Turn into Action

One morning in Boston, Massachusetts, a young man got into an argument with a British guard at the *customs house*, where taxes were paid. More people gathered around the customs house. After many angry words, British soldiers fired their guns.

Five men lay dead in the snow-covered street. Eight were wounded. Crispus Attucks, a free black man, was one of the men killed. He was the first African American to die for the cause of freedom in America. This event is known as the Boston Massacre.

The Boston Tea Party

The colonists were so angry about the tea tax that they decided to teach England a lesson. In Boston, men dressed up like American Indians and went to the harbor. They went on board British ships and dumped all the tea into the water. This event is called the Boston Tea Party.

The colonists dumped crates full of British tea into Boston Harbor. Some of the other colonies held their own "tea parties."

The British government punished the people of Boston. It closed the port until the colonists paid for the spoiled tea. Boston was a busy trading city at this time. Closing the port meant the people could not work or make money there. Some had a hard time buying food because they couldn't earn money.

The people of Connecticut wanted to help the people of Boston. One day, people were lining up along the streets of Boston. Something was coming! Soon a short old man came int view. He was bringing a flock of 125 sheep to feed the people. The man was Israel Putnam, a farmer from Pomfret. He was a member of the Sons of Liberty.

The Colonists Come Together

The colonists decided to start working together as a team. Every colony except Georgia sent men to a meeting in Philadelphi Pennsylvania, to talk about their problems with the British. The meeting was called the First Continental Congress.

Back in Connecticut, people started collecting guns and *ammunition* to get ready for whatever would happen next. At the same time, England was sending more soldiers and ships to America. They would be ready if fighting broke out.

The Fighting Begins

British soldiers marched toward Concord, Massachusetts. Their goal was to find and destroy anything that might be used to start a war against them. They looked for guns, powder, lea to make bullets, and anything else the colonists might be hiding

Soldiers carried their bullets in a bullet box like this one.
(Photo by Jean Crossman, Courtesy of the Amherst History Museum)

When the British reached Lexington, on the way to Concord, they were met by armed men from the local militia. Suddenly a shot rang out. Who fired it? Neither side admitted it. Then more shots were fired. When the smoke cleared, eight Americans were dead and ten were wounded. That first shot is known as the "shot heard 'round the world."

The British moved on and searched the buildings in Lexington and Concord. More shots were fired at Concord. Th Revolutionary War had begun.

The Connecticut Adventu

The Colonies Send Help

The other colonies sent men to Massachusetts to help fight the British. Connecticut men went to join the ranks. Israel Putnam urged leaders in the towns around him to send men. He rode his horse all night to reach Cambridge, where soldiers were gathering. He joined them and got ready to fight. Soon more groups of men from Connecticut arrived.

The British Are Coming!

The people at Lexington and Concord knew the British were coming. How did they know? Paul Revere and two other men, William Dawes and Samuel Prescott, had warned them the night before. Paul Revere had watched the troops set out from Boston. He and the other two men rode their horses all night to tell the colonists to get ready.

Colonists and British soldiers met at Concord Bridge. Americans called the British "Redcoats" or "Lobster-Backs." Why do you think the colonists chose these names?

Declaring Independence

Once the fighting had begun, more Americans wanted to break away from England and start their own country. Men from all of the colonies met again in Philadelphia. This meeting was called the Second Continental Congress.

The men voted to declare independence from England. Thomas Jefferson of Virginia was asked to write a letter to the

"Don't fire until you see the whites of their eyes!"

—Israel Putnam

Hannah Bunce Watson
1750–?

Hannah Bunce Watson and Ebenezer Watson owned *The Connecticut Courant*. It was one of the oldest and largest newspapers in the colonies. It kept everyone in the colonies informed when the British shut down the Boston papers.

Hannah was busy caring for five young children. Then her husband got sick and died. With the help of an assistant, Hannah took over the paper. She became one of the first female editors in the colonies.

Hannah worked very hard to save the newspaper after a fire struck the mill where the paper was made. Her work paid off, and the paper never missed an issue.

The Connecticut Courant became *The Hartford Courant*. It is still around today.

British king. The letter said that, because they had been treated unfairly, the American colonies were cutting all ties with Great Britain. On July 4, 1776, the letter was ready.

Delegates from all the thirteen colonies signed the letter. We call it the Declaration of Independence.

The men from Connecticut who signed the Declaration of Independence were Samuel Huntington, Roger Sherman, William Williams, and Oliver Wolcott.

The colonies were on their way to becoming independent states, but it was not going to be easy.

Read All about It!

Newspapers helped people know what was going on during this troubled time. The first newspaper in the colony was *The Connecticut Gazette*. A few years later, other newspapers started bringing news to the colonists.

Most newspapers carried news from places such as London and New York. There were two or three columns of advertising each week. There were also articles about farming, mathematics, and *astronomy* (the study of the planets and stars).

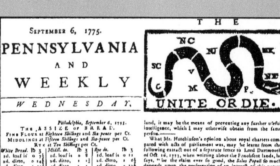

After the Declaration of Independence was signed, it was printed in newspapers or read aloud in all of the colonies. The people of Connecticut read it in The Connecticut Courant. Can you find any of the men from Connecticut who signed the paper?

The Struggle for Independence

The Provisions State

Now that the colonies were at war, the soldiers needed clothes, food, and shelter. They had to have guns and bullets. Connecticut's most important role during the war was in giving the soldiers the supplies they needed. Connecticut sent so many supplies, or *provisions*, to the soldiers that it became known as the Provisions State.

Soldiers slept in small cabins or huts. Sometimes they had to sleep on the ground.

Food and Clothing

Women made clothing for the soldiers. They nursed the sick and made bandages for the wounded. While their husbands, brothers, and sons were off fighting the British, women kept everything going at home.

Connecticut provided beef and pork for the soldiers to eat. Each week, a soldier received:

- three-quarters of a pound of pork or one pound of beef
- one pound of bread or flour
- tobacco and three pints of beer
- rum, milk, molasses, vinegar, coffee, chocolate, sugar, and vegetables
- soap and candles

The Connecticut Adventu

"Brother Jonathan"

Governor Jonathan Trumbull worked hard to give his soldiers everything they needed. The troops spent a very cold winter at Valley Forge, Pennsylvania. The men were freezing and hungry. He asked men to round up cattle to be sent to Valley Forge. Because of Jonathan Trumbull, Connecticut soldiers were not as bad off as many others.

George Washington came to rely on the Connecticut governor. Whenever he needed supplies, he said, "We must consult Brother Jonathan." Washington wrote to him:

> *Among the troops unfit for duty and returned for want of clothing, none of your state are included. The care . . . in providing clothing . . . for their men . . . reflects the greatest honor upon their patriotism and humanity.*

Jonathan Trumbull helped Washington again during a horrible winter in New Jersey. Again he sent food and supplies to the starving, freezing army.

Jonathan Trumbull worked hard to get more men to join the army. He offered rewards to get enough men to sign up.

Weapons and Troops

In addition to food and clothing, Connecticut provided gunpowder, weapons, and troops. The General Assembly offered a reward for people who would make gunpowder. Soon people in East Hartford, Windham, New Haven, and Salisbury were making gunpowder. Craftsmen in Mansfield, Windham, and Goshen started making more guns. In Salisbury, a factory made cannons for the forts and ships along Connecticut's coast.

Connecticut Portrait

Jonathan Trumbull
1710–1785

Jonathan Trumbull studied to become a minister, but he became a merchant instead. He lived in the town of Lebanon. He helped his town by starting a library and a private school there.

Trumbull served in the General Assembly, then became a judge. He was elected deputy (assistant) governor and then governor of Connecticut.

Trumbull was a good leader and patriot during the *revolution*. He helped his country by giving the army large amounts of food and supplies.

Jonathan Trumbull was married to Faith Robinson. They had four sons and two daughters. Their youngest son, John, was an artist. He painted many scenes of the American Revolution. His paintings are now on display in the Capitol Building in Washington, D.C.

Patriots and Loyalists

Not all of the colonists wanted to break away from England. Some wanted to stay loyal to the king. They were called *loyalists*.

Those who wanted independence were called *patriots*. Every colony had both groups. Some families were split between the two groups.

Nathan Hale
A Connecticut Hero

Family Life

Nathan Hale came from a large family. He had eleven brothers and sisters. When he was just fourteen, he entered Yale College. After graduating, he became a schoolteacher in East Haddam and New London.

From Schoolteacher to Hero

When the Revolutionary War broke out, Nathan Hale went to join the troops. He was later promoted to captain. He became friends with General George Washington.

Washington's troops were in trouble. They were outnumbered by the British. They had few supplies. Washington needed information about the British plans. He needed someone to go behind British lines as a spy.

Nathan Hale understood the danger. He also understood how important it was to defeat the British. He volunteered for the mission.

Dressed as a schoolteacher, Hale crossed enemy lines. He secretly made sketches of the British forts. He made notes about how many there were and where they were located.

General Washington and Nathan Hale work out their plan.

On his way back, someone recognized Hale. He was taken to the British for questioning. When they found the papers hidden on him, he admitted that he was a spy.

Nathan Hale was ordered to be hanged the next morning. Before dying, he spoke these famous last words:

"I only regret that I have but one life to lose for my country."

An officer who was there told what happened that day:

'Captain Hale entered: he was calm, and bore himself with gentle dignity. . . . He asked for writing materials, . . . he wrote two letters, one to his mother and one to a brother officer. He was shortly [called] to the gallows. But a few persons were around him, yet his . . . dying words were remembered.'

—recorded by Captain William Hull

Nathan Hale says his famous last words.

More than 200 years later, Nathan Hale became Connecticut's official state hero.

What do you think?

What did Nathan Hale mean when he said, "I only regret that I have but one life to lose for my country"? Why did these words make him a hero?

Benedict Arnold—from Hero to Traitor

Early in the war, Captain Benedict Arnold from Norwich led a group of Connecticut men to join the army. At first, he was a hero. He captured British forts and led brave attacks. Everyone thought he was a great commander. But their opinion of him was about to change.

Benedict Arnold was put in charge of an American fort in New York. He became friends with the leader of the British Army. The British said they would pay Arnold a lot of money and make him a leader in the British Army if he would turn over the fort to them. Benedict Arnold took their offer.

When people discovered what Arnold had done, they went after him. He escaped and joined the British side, but he became known as a *traitor*. Today, we often call a disloyal person a "Benedict Arnold."

Benedict Arnold escapes!

Nero Hawley

Some slaves fought in the Revolutionary War. As a reward, many were freed at the end of the war. Nero Hawley was a slave in the town of Trumbull. He joined the American army.

Nero Hawley fought in battles and was with the soldiers at Valley Forge. He survived the war and went back to live in Trumbull as a free man. Today you can visit Nero Hawley's grave in Trumbull.

Nero Hawley was buried in Trumbull. Does your town's cemetery have graves of anyone from revolutionary times?

Battles in Connecticut

Several battles took place in Connecticut. British soldiers raided Danbury, where the colonists kept guns. The British collected as much as they could. They burned the storage buildings and some of the town. They destroyed the corn crops.

Two days later, Americans attacked at Ridgefield. The British escaped in ships on Long Island Sound. However, they lost a lot of men.

The following winter, the British led an attack on Greenwich. Connecticut soldiers drove the British away, but the town suffered a lot of damage.

In July, the British went through New Haven, burning and destroying property. They burned over 200 buildings in Fairfield. In Norwalk, they destroyed churches, shops, houses, barns, flour mills, and ships. Children heard gunfire and saw the smoke. They were very frightened.

In the last battle on Connecticut soil, Benedict Arnold led British soldiers in a raid on New London and Groton. It was a bloody battle. Finally the Americans surrendered, but the British were still very angry. When the American commander held out his sword to surrender, a British officer grabbed the sword and ran it through the commander's body. The British troops took up their swords and killed about eighty more Americans.

Connecticut at Sea

Connecticut's location on the water made it important during the war. Warships came in and out of many Connecticut ports. New London was the busiest port.

Connecticut even built its own small navy. The Connecticut *fleet* had the important job of protecting our coast. Before the war ended, thirteen ships had served in this navy.

There was even a small submarine called the *American Turtle*. David Bushnell of Saybrook had designed it. It looked like the shells of two turtles.

Merchants and ship owners could not do their usual work during the war. They were called upon to attack and capture British ships. These sailors were called *privateers*. The privateers captured nearly 500 British ships.

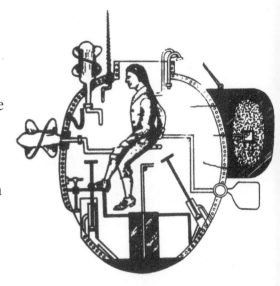

Inside the first submarine, a sailor turned propellers that pushed the boat through the water. The submarine moved close to a British ship. The sailor attached a wooden crate filled with gunpowder to the ship. After the submarine moved away, the gunpowder exploded like a bomb.

This painting shows the American Turtle *at sea. Do you think it looks like a turtle?*

Victory!

Americans needed help fighting the British. They asked France to help them. With the help of the French, the war finally ended. Over 5,000 soldiers and a great fleet of ships arrived from France. The French also lent the Americans money to buy food, clothing, and weapons, and to pay the soldiers.

Plans for the last American victory were made in Wethersfield. Washington and the French generals planned to attack the British in the Chesapeake Bay area. While they were doing this, the British general moved his troops to Yorktown, Virginia. French ships blocked the entrance to the river there. They cut off any chance of the soldiers getting help from British ships.

The British general surrendered to General Washington. The Revolutionary War was over.

About 40,000 men from Connecticut served in the Revolutionary War.

Activity

Looking at Old Newspapers

In the days before radio, television, and computers, newspapers kept people informed. Read these items printed in colonial newspapers. Notice the interesting word choice and spelling.

1. Did you ever have to go to the "lost and found" in your school? Read this item printed on February 9, 1764 in *The Pennsylvania Gazette*.

"Found, a Silver Watch, on the Great Road leading from Haddonfield to Glouster, the 21st of January last. The Owner, proving his property, and paying Charges, may have it again, by applying to Benjamin Sykes, living in Chesterfield, Burlington County."

- What do you think the "Charges" might be?
- Does Mr. Sykes have a street address? How will the owner locate him?

2. Here is a news item that appeared in *The American Weekly Mercury* in 1737.

"The Ice in the River Delaware remains yet and People continue to pass over it but 'tis now becomes so rotten that several Men and Horses have broke through and narrowly escap'd drowning."

- How do people cross rivers today?
- Do they have to wait for the river to freeze before they can cross over it?

Chapter 5 Review

1. Why did England tax the colonies?

2. Why did the colonists think the taxes were unfair?

3. Why were newspapers important during the Revolution?

4. What Connecticut woman edited *The Connecticut Courant*?

5. Which Connecticut men signed the Declaration of Independence?

6. How did Connecticut help in the war effort?

7. Who did George Washington call "Brother Jonathan"?

8. What did "Brother Jonathan" do?

9. Who is Connecticut's most famous Revolutionary War hero?
   (Hint: He is our state hero today.)

10. What famous traitor came from Connecticut?

11. List three Connecticut towns that were attacked by the British.

12. What European country helped the Americans win the Revolutionary War?

Geography Tie-In

Why were the port cities, such as New London and Groton, so important in a time of war?

The Struggle for Independence

PEOPLE TO KNOW
Alexander Hamilton
Roger Sherman
William Samuel Johnson
Oliver Ellsworth
James Madison
George Washington
Noah Webster

PLACES TO LOCATE
West Hartford
Essex
Stonington
Philadelphia, Pennsylvania
Virginia
New York
New Jersey
England

Our Role in the

1775–1783
Revolutionary War

1791
The Bill of Rights is added
to the Constitution.

Timeline of Events   1775   1780   1785   1790

1776
The Declaration of
Independence is
signed.

1780
Noah Webster
publishes a spelling
book of American
English.

1787
The U.S. Constitution is written.
Connecticut is the fifth state to sign
the Constitution.
Connecticut becomes a state.

New Nation

6

WORDS TO UNDERSTAND
amendment
compromise
democracy
House of Representatives
legislator
monarchy
political party
ratify
representative democracy
Senate

*George Washington leads the
Founding Fathers as they write
the Constitution.*

795	1800	1805	1810	1815	1820

1796
e Old State House is
built in Hartford.

1818
Connecticut approves a
new state constitution.

From Colonies to United States

Once Americans were free of England's control, the country needed a set of laws to live by. The people did not want a *monarchy*. They did not want a king, a queen, or a prince to have all of the power. They wanted a way to rule themselves. They wanted a *democracy*.

So far, things were not going well. Each state had its own government. Each had its own kind of money. No one knew how much a Virginia coin was worth compared to a Connecticut coin. This made it hard for people to buy things from people in other states.

The national government was not strong enough to solve these and other problems. The leaders of America knew something had to be done.

Alexander Hamilton of New York sent out a message to important men in each state. He asked them to come to a meeting to solve these problems so they could be a strong country, not just a group of states.

Alexander Hamilton

The Constitutional Convention

It was a hot, sticky summer in Philadelphia. Outside Independence Hall, the bees were buzzing, and the sun was beating down through the windows. Inside the building, men were working. Even in the hot weather, they kept the windows closed so that no one outside could hear what they were saying.

What was the big meeting about? Why was everything such a secret? The men who were talking, arguing, and writing inside Independence Hall were delegates who had come from twelve states to write the Constitution. It would set up a government

for the new United States of America. The meeting, which lasted all summer, was called the Constitutional Convention.

Three delegates from Connecticut were at the meeting. They
were William Samuel Johnson, Roger Sherman, and Oliver
Ellsworth.

*At Independence Hall in Philadelphia, the U.S. Constitution was written
and a new kind of government was born.*

William Samuel Johnson

Roger Sherman

Oliver Ellsworth

Linking the past to the present

At the Constitutional Convention, no one from the public
was allowed to know what the men were saying until the
meeting was over. That way, the delegates could experiment
with different ideas and speak freely about them.

Today, many of our government meetings and courtrooms
have TV cameras in them. Everyone in America can see and
hear what is going on as it happens.

Do you think there are good reasons to keep some government meetings secret? Should the people be allowed to
know everything that goes on in their government?

Connecticut Portrait

Roger Sherman
1721–1793

Roger Sherman was already well known in Connecticut when he was chosen to go to the Constitutional Convention. He had worked as a shoemaker, then as a lawyer, a judge, and a congressman. He had signed the Declaration of Independence.

Roger Sherman played an important role at the Constitutional Convention. He spoke more than any other delegate except James Madison. He also suggested the Connecticut Compromise, which ended a long argument between the states.

After signing the U.S. Constitution, Roger Sherman served as the mayor of New Haven.

A Time to Compromise

The delegates did not know they were in for such a long summer. This was the first time people had met to make a government that the people themselves would run. It was hard to convince each state to give up some of its power and follow the rules of a national government.

The delegates all wanted to make their new country a republic, or *representative democracy*. That means the people elect representatives to make the laws for them. The people still have the power. If the representatives don't vote the way the people want them to, the people can vote for someone else next time.

The men debated about how representatives would be chosen. The big states wanted more voting power. The smaller states thought that wasn't fair. They wanted each state to be equal when they voted.

The Virginia Plan

Virginia was one of the largest states. The delegates from Virginia said that the number of representatives from a state should be based on how many people lived there. This was known as the Virginia Plan.

The New Jersey Plan

The delegates from New Jersey said that each state should have the same number of representatives. They wanted smaller states like Connecticut, Delaware, and Rhode Island to have the same number of representatives as the larger states. This was known as the New Jersey Plan.

The Connecticut Compromise

Roger Sherman had an idea for a *compromise* between the two plans. He worked with the other men from Connecticut on the Connecticut Compromise. The Connecticut Compromise set up two groups, or houses, in Congress.

In one group, called the *Senate*, each state would have two senators, no matter how many people lived there. This would be fair to the smaller states.

In the other group, called the *House of Representatives*, each state would have one or more representatives, according to how many people lived there. Larger states would have more representatives than smaller states, so all the people were represented.

When the delegates counted all the people who needed to be represented, they did not count slaves the same as other people. They agreed that five slaves would equal three white men.

What do you think?

Pretend your class is voting on how long recess should be. Your teacher tells you that everyone with a blue shirt will only count as three-fifths of a vote. Everyone else will count as one vote. If you are wearing a blue shirt, how do you feel? Do you think the slaves thought the three-fifths rule was fair?

The Constitution was written and rewritten.
The men chose each word carefully.
They tried to make a Constitution that
would be strong even in the future.
(Drawing by Gary Rasmussen)

Balancing the Power

The delegates finally agreed that one government that made laws, set up taxes, and had certain powers over all the states was the best idea. But many people didn't like the idea of a national government. England had given them an example of what could happen when a government has too much power over its people.

To make sure just one person or a few people would not have all the power, the power of government was split three ways.

The three parts, or branches, of government are:

• **Legislative:** The legislative branch makes the laws. It is the United States Congress.

• **Executive:** The executive branch makes sure the laws are carried out. It is the president, vice president, and their cabinet (helpers).

• **Judicial:** The judicial branch says what the laws mean. It decides if a person has broken a law. It is the Supreme Court and other federal courts.

A Lasting Constitution

In the end, the men were able to work out their differences. They came up with a constitution for the country. It was a great achievement, and it officially formed the government of the thirteen states.

Another important thing came from the Constitutional Convention—the country got a new name. Everyone agreed to call it the United States of America.

Connecticut Approves

Each state had to *ratify*, or sign, the new Constitution. A few months after it was written, the Constitution was printed in the newspaper. In towns around the state, people discussed it.

Oliver Ellsworth wrote some letters under the name of "A Landholder." The letters argued that the Constitution would make the United States a strong country. Roger Sherman also

George Washington was elected to be the first president of the United States of America.

wrote letters to newspapers saying how important it was to have a strong national government.

Like many other states, Connecticut held its own small convention to discuss the Constitution. Delegates were chosen from each town in Connecticut. The delegates met at the Old State House in Hartford in the cold month of January. The Old State House was so cold that they quickly moved to the First Meeting House, which was heated.

People could come and listen to the meetings. Newspapers printed the debates. When the vote was taken, 128 men voted to sign the Constitution. There were only 40 votes against it. Connecticut was the fifth state to ratify the Constitution.

James Madison was a delegate from Virginia. He is called the "Father of the Constitution" because he provided so many of the ideas that formed our government.

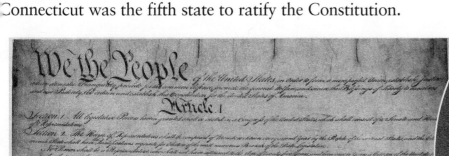

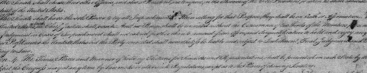

The paper has yellowed and faded, but the words of the Constitution are still the basis for our government today. Can you read the first three words? Why are they important?

Branches of Government

The branches of government worked so well that we still have them today. Look at the giant government treehouse to review what you have learned about government and see how it applies to us today.

Legislative Branch

The men and women elected to make our laws are our representatives. They are also called *legislators.* On the legislative branch, find the people who are debating and giving speeches about what laws they want to be passed. Find the people who travel back and forth to the executive branch to get laws made.

Executive Branch

The executive branch carries out the laws. The president is head of the country's executive branch. Find the reporters asking questions. Find the people trying to come in to talk with the president. Find the guard outside the room.

Judicial Branch

The courts make up the judicial branch. Courts decide what the laws mean. They try to settle problems in a peaceful way.

A jury is a group of people who listen to cases and decide if a person is innocent or guilty. A judge listens to the person on trial and decides what the punishment should be.

Find the judge, jury, and court reporter. The court reporter writes down everything that is said in court.

(Drawing by Jon Burton)

Constitution and Bill of Rights

Our government is based on our Constitution. It is the most important document in the whole United States. The Bill of Rights is also very important. It states that our government cannot make laws to take away our freedoms of speech or religion. Talk with your teacher and your class about other rights in the Bill of Rights.

Political Parties

Political parties are groups of people who share many of the same ideas about government and what it should do for the people. The main parties today are the Democrats and Republicans. Find the elephant at the base of the tree. It represents the Republicans. Now find the donkey. It represents the Democrats.

Voting

The most important thing to remember about our government is that its leaders represent all of us. Find the people voting for their leaders. Then find those leaders climbing up the tree to serve in one of the branches of government.

Connecticut Portrait

Noah Webster
1758–1843

Have you ever used *Webster's Dictionary* to look up a word you didn't know? Noah Webster started writing dictionaries a long time ago. He was a patriot from West Hartford who had served in the revolution.

America was forming its own government, and Noah thought America should have its own language. Even though Americans spoke English, they spoke their own kind of English. For example, the word "centre" became "center." American words such as "skunk" and "pecan" were not in spelling books. Noah put these and other American words into *Webster's Elementary Spelling Book*. Many schools used it to teach spelling.

Later, Noah wrote *The American Dictionary of the English Language*. He also wrote about the government and started several newspapers.

The Bill of Rights

When the first U.S. Congress met, they decided to add something to the Constitution. They agreed that it was important to spell out just what the people's rights were. They wanted to make sure their rights were protected so that no one could take them away.

They added ten changes, or **amendments**, to the Constitution. The amendments were called the Bill of Rights. It listed the rights of each citizen. Some of the rights were the right to belong to any religion, to speak freely, and to write and print whatever people thought was important. These were rights that people in many other countries did not have.

The War of 1812

The years passed, and the United States was still having trouble with England. The two countries argued over land and trading rights. Soon the United States was thinking about fighting another war with England.

The people of Connecticut belonged to political parties, just like we do today. Most people in Connecticut belonged to a political party called the Federalists. The Federalists were against going to war with England again.

Connecticut and the other New England states sent men to Hartford to talk about whether or not they would go to war. This meeting is known as the Hartford Convention.

At War Again

The United States did go to war with England again in 1812. Some of the battles took place in Connecticut. About 200 British sailors sailed up the Connecticut River to the port of Essex. They destroyed about twenty small ships. At Stonington, the British commander gave

he people in the town one hour to leave before he started
ombing. The people refused to leave. For three days the
British bombed Stonington. Only one American was wounded,
ut the damage to the town was great.

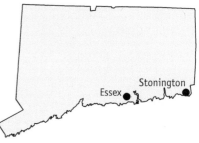

*Isaac Hull of Shelton
was commander of the
American ship, the* USS
Constitution. *The ship
had strong sides that
held up well against
British bombs. The ship
was nicknamed "Old
Ironsides."*

A New State Constitution

The Charter of 1662 was still the state law in Connecticut. However, by 1818, times had changed. The people of Connecticut wanted a new state constitution.

On the Fourth of July, the people held town meetings across the state. They chose delegates to go to a convention at the Old State House. The delegates wrote a new constitution for the state.

The new constitution changed several things. The most important change was that all churches, not just the Congregational Church, would be accepted.

The people of Connecticut approved the new constitution on October 5, 1818. It is known as the Constitution of 1818.

"All Men Are Created Equal"

Little by little, Connecticut ended slavery. A new law said that every African American born after 1784 would be free at the age of twenty-five. This was better than being a slave for life, but black children still had to wait many years for their freedom.

A few years after the law was passed, the president of Yale helped start the first anti-slavery society in Connecticut. Members of the society worked to convince people around the country that slavery was wrong.

Activity

A Class Constitution

Together with your classmates, write a class constitution. Here are some questions to get you started:

- What are "rights"?
- What rights do you and your classmates enjoy most?
- What laws can you write to protect your rights?
- What are the laws you agree to live by in the classroom?

Remember, you may have to compromise just like the delegates did. Write up your constitution, and then take a vote to see if everyone approves it. As time goes by, you may need to add some changes, or amendments.

Chapter 6 Review

1. A government in which one person, such as a king or queen, rules is called a _____.
2. A government in which the people vote for their leaders is called a _____.
3. What three men represented Connecticut at the Constitutional Convention?
4. Explain the difference between the New Jersey Plan and the Virginia Plan.
5. How did the Connecticut Compromise bring peace to the Constitutional Convention?
6. Did slaves get to vote in the new government? Explain your answer.
7. Who was the first president of the United States?
8. What is the Bill of Rights?
9. Why was the Bill of Rights added to the Constitution?
10. When did Connecticut get a new state constitution?

Geography Tie-In

1. Find Pennsylvania on the map of the thirteen colonies. Why did its location make it a good place for the delegates to meet and write the U.S. Constitution?

2. What colonies did delegates from Connecticut have to travel through to reach Pennsylvania?

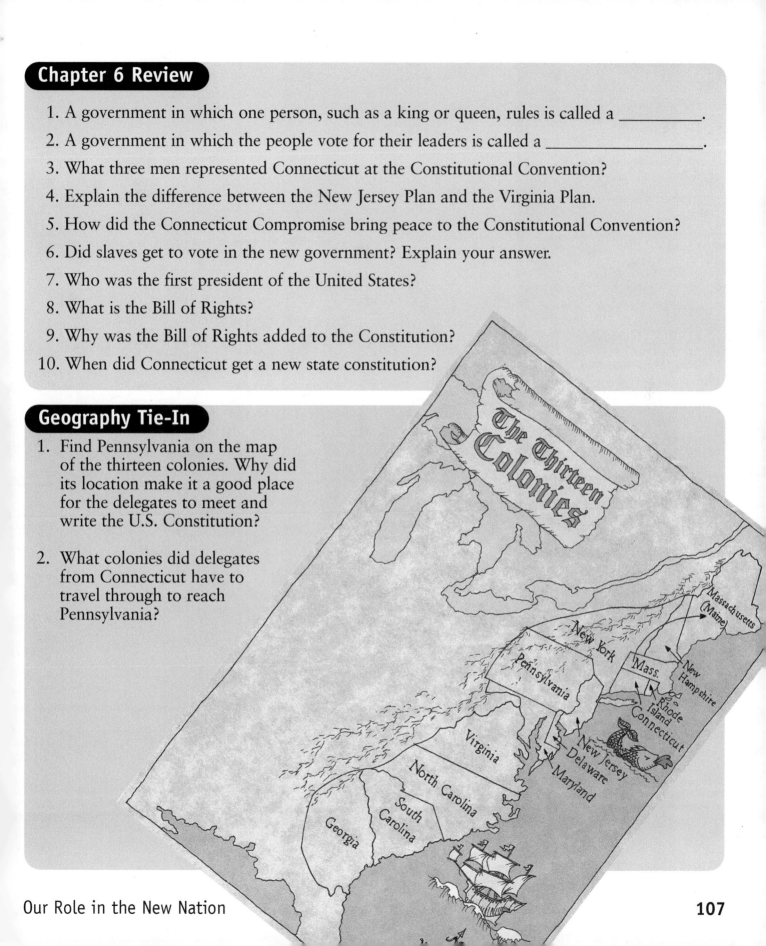

The Thirteen Colonies

Our Role in the New Nation

Chapter 7

THE TIME
1790–1850

PEOPLE TO KNOW
David Humphreys
Eli Whitney
Samuel Colt
Joseph Lawrence
Gerson Fox
Thomas Gallaudet
Eli Todd
Henry Barnard
James W. C. Pennington
Emma Hart Willard
Sarah Porter
Catherine Beecher
Lydia Howard Sigourney
Prudence Crandall

PLACES TO LOCATE
Canterbury
Berlin
Waterbury
Derby
New Haven
Hamden
Hartford
East Windsor
New London
Stonington
Mystic
Granby
Connecticut River
Naugatuck River
Ohio
England
Scotland
Germany
Ireland

1791
Eli Whitney invents the cotton gin.

1794
The first insurance companies open in Hartford.

1790
The first anti-slavery society in Connecticut meets.

1792
The first turnpike company is started.

Chapter 7

Industry Brings Change

WORDS TO UNDERSTAND
abolitionist
canal
economy
heroine
immigrant
Industrial Revolution
insurance
interchangeable
mass production
raw materials
reform
rural
tenement
textile
toll

In the mills, girls worked the power looms. The looms wove thread into cloth. They were powered by the rushing water of a nearby river.

1817
Thomas Gallaudet opens the American School for the Deaf.

1833
Prudence Crandall starts the first school for African American girls in New England.

1835
The Farmington Canal is built.

1840s
The whaling industry reaches its high point.

1820   1830   1840   1850

1826
Connecticut's first African American church opens in New Haven.

1838
Railroad tracks connect New Haven and Hartford.

1844
A railroad line connects New Haven to New York City.

Westward, Ho!

After the revolution, many young families packed up their belongings and headed to other parts of the country. One reason they left was because the best farmland already had been taken by earlier settlers. They wanted to find good land to farm.

Some families left for religious reasons. They wanted to live in an area where the Congregational Church was not so powerful.

Some families settled in western Massachusetts. Others went to Vermont or New Hampshire. The settlers often gave their new town the same name as the town they had come from. That is why Vermont has towns named Andover, Berlin, Bloomfield, Burlington, Cornwall, Fairfield, Granby, Groton, and Guilford—just like Connecticut.

Many families moved into the Western Reserve. The Western Reserve was a large area of land that later became the state of Ohio. Moses Cleveland was a pioneer from Canterbury. The town he started became Cleveland, Ohio.

This pioneer house was built of logs in Ohio in 1798.

Why do you think pioneers traveled in covered wagons? They needed the wagons to carry the things they would need in their new home. Most of the time, the older children had to walk beside the wagon. If it rained or they had to rest, they could climb inside.

From the Farm to the Factory

Some people stopped farming for a living. They started going to the larger towns and cities to work in new industries. Men, women, and children left the farms to work in factories.

Machines had been invented in Europe that could make things faster than people could make them by hand. This was called the *Industrial Revolution.* Factories and mills that needed hundreds of machines were built.

Soon the Industrial Revolution came to Connecticut. In Berlin, workers made tin. In Waterbury, they made buttons and brass. In Derby, they worked in the wool industry. David Humphreys brought sheep over from Spain. He started a company that made wool cloth. Wool, cotton, and paper mills opened around the state. Ironware, shoes, stagecoaches, glass, pottery, guns, clocks, and hats were made in Connecticut.

Banks and Insurance

With all the new business, people needed a place to keep their money. Banks were started in Hartford and New London. The first insurance companies opened in Hartford and Norwich.

Insurance is money that is paid to a company who will pay the costs if something bad happens. Today, Hartford is called the "Insurance Capital of the World."

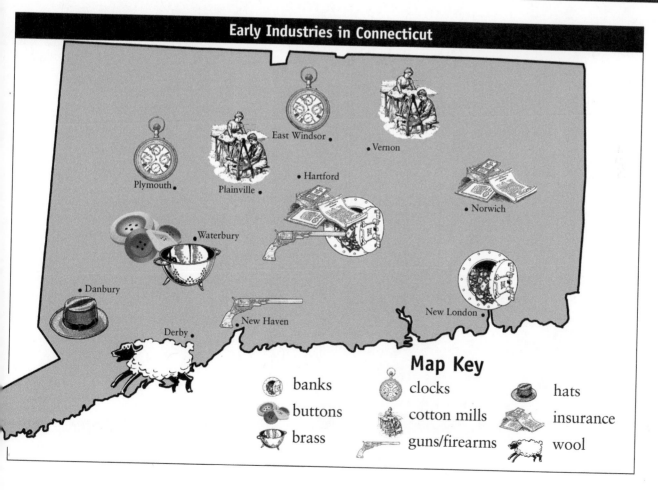

Early Industries in Connecticut

East Windsor •
• Vernon
Plymouth •
Plainville •
• Hartford
Waterbury •
• Norwich
• Danbury
New London •
Derby •
• New Haven

Map Key

banks   clocks   hats
buttons   cotton mills   insurance
brass   guns/firearms   wool

Eli Whitney

1765–1825

Hamden
New Haven

E li Whitney left New Haven and went to stay at a Georgia cotton plantation. While he was helping the plantation owner, he noticed how long it took the workers and slaves to clean the cotton. It took many hours to remove the tiny cotton seeds from the cotton fibers by hand.

Eli had always understood how machines worked. He wanted to invent a machine to clean cotton. He watched the workers carefully. He studied their hand movements as they worked.

After much hard work and thought, Eli made a machine to do the work. He called it the cotton gin. The cotton gin could clean more cotton in one hour than several workers could clean in a whole day.

Cotton soon became the most important crop in the South. Eli and the plantation owner started a factory to build cotton gins in New Haven.

"He can make anything."
—Mrs. Catharine Green

Years later, Eli started making guns and other firearms. He agreed to make 10,000 muskets for the government. He built a factory in what is now Hamden.

In Eli's new factory, each machine made a certain part of the musket. The parts could fit any of the muskets he produced. This is called a system of **interchangeable** parts. It was a much faster way to make things.

Many people followed Eli Whitney's way of making muskets. They used interchangeable parts to make clocks, tools, and much later, automobiles.

Cotton took hours to clean by hand. The cotton gin could clean it in minutes.

By 1870, almost half of the people working in Connecticut worked in a factory.

"There was but one summer holiday for us who worked in the mills—the Fourth of July. We made a point of spending it out of doors, making [outings] down the river . . . or around by the old canal path."

—*Lucy Larcom,*
A New England Girlhood

*Women and children worked alongside men in the **textile** mills. They fed the cotton or wool into the machines. The machines wove the threads into cloth. Then the workers folded the finished cloth.*

Mass Production

Machines were helping factory workers make many goods at once, instead of one at a time. This is called mass production. People in Connecticut began to mass produce their products. Then they could sell more and make more money.

Samuel Colt invented the "six-shooter." It was a handgun that could hold six bullets instead of one. He used Eli Whitney's system of interchangeable parts to make it. He also used machines, rather than craftsmen, to produce his guns.

For his new factory, Colt bought land along the Connecticut River in Hartford. He made the outside of his factory very fancy, so that boat passengers on the Connecticut River would notice it. Today, drivers on I-91 still see it.

Another gun factory was started by Horace Smith and Daniel Wesson. They invented a new kind of rifle called the Winchester. It was made in both New Haven and in Springfield, Massachusetts.

Colt Paterson

Eli Terry of East Windsor used mass production to make clocks. He used the water-power of the Naugatuck River to run his machines. The machines made the parts for the clocks.

This was the sign for Nathan Ruggles' business. He made looking glasses (mirrors). According to the sign, what else did he make?

You can see how mass production started in this shoe shop. Each person makes a part of the shoe. Then the shoe is passed to the next person. Find the man who is cutting the leather. What jobs are the other men doing?

Industry Brings Change

"There she blows!" shouted the crew members when they spotted a whale. Most hunting crews included a captain, sailors, harpooners, a cook, a steward (officer in charge of supplies), a cooper (person who made wooden barrels), a blacksmith, an engineer, and a cabin boy who cleaned up.

Sailing around the world to hunt whales was an adventure!

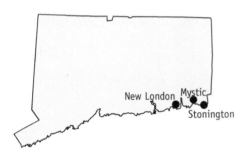

A Whale of a Business

One of the biggest industries in Connecticut during this time was the whaling industry. Brave men left ports such as New London, Stonington, and Mystic. They sailed across the ocean for many months in search of whales.

Whaling was a very dangerous job. Usually, the whale was much larger than the ship. Once the men had spotted a whale, they climbed into smaller boats and rowed towards the whale. They had to get close enough to aim and throw their harpoons.

Once they killed a whale, they tied it to the ship. Then they cut off the parts they wanted and left the rest in the ocean. Sharks often came and ate the rest of the whale.

The crew brought back oil from the whales. Whale oil was used to make perfume and to light lamps in houses, steam trains, lighthouses, and streets. The oil burned brightly and gave off less smoke than other oils. Countries such as England, France, and Spain bought a lot of whale oil.

Most of the men who owned the whaling ships came from old New England families. But Giuseppe Lorenzo came from

taly. He changed his name to Joseph Lawrence. He made his
amily very wealthy. With some of their money, the family start-
:d a hospital in New London that is still helping people today.

Transportation Helps Industry

People wanted to sell their new products in other parts of
:he state and country. They wanted to bring in raw materials
and goods that were not found in Connecticut. They needed a
better system of transportation.

Better Roads

The first roads were just packed-down dirt. Traveling on
:hem was slow and bumpy. When it rained, the roads turned to
nud. Wagons and carriages got stuck.

The first turnpike company hired
workers to build the Mohegan Road
between New London and Norwich.
The Mohegan Road was a **toll** road.
Everyone who used the road had to
:top and pay a fee. The money
helped to keep the road clean
and safe.

The people rode in stagecoaches
or wagons pulled by horses. Many
people just walked or rode a horse.

Travelers on the Hartford &
New Haven Turnpike watched for
:ed stone markers. The markers
showed them how many more
miles they had to go. That's
why the markers are called
milestones.

You can learn all about life in
an old whaling village if you
visit Mystic Seaport.
(Photo by Kindra Clineff)

*These turnpike tickets were sold
on the Hartford & New Haven
Turnpike. How much did it cost
for three large animals to pass?
How much did it cost for a loaded
wagon, sled, and sleigh to pass?*

Canals

It was faster and easier to travel on the water than on land, but the rivers didn't go everywhere that people wanted to go. To solve this problem, the people built canals. A *canal* is a man-made waterway. Canals were built to connect a river to another river, or a river to a lake or ocean. Then people could follow an all-water route.

The most important canal in Connecticut was the Farmington Canal. Merchants wanted a route to towns in the Connecticut River Valley. Workers began digging, and in ten years, boats were traveling from New Haven to Massachusetts.

A mule on a towpath pulled a boat through the canal.
(Photo by John Ivanko)

A special kind of boat worked best on the canals. Canal boats had flat bottoms. They did not have engines. Mules or horses on the bank pulled them with heavy ropes. Many young boys wanted the job of leading the mule down the towpath.

At first it seemed like canals would be a big success, but rail roads were soon invented. The proved to be a better way for people and goods to travel.

Railroads

Many people traveled between Boston and New York. Connecticut wanted some of that traffic so it could get more business. In 1837, tracks were layed from Rhode Island to Stonington. At Stonington, people could get off the train and ride a steamship to New York City. Soon other railroad lines were built. New Haven and Hartford were connected by rail. A few years later, there was a line from New Haven to New York City.

The railroads brought more people from the *rural* areas to the cities. They made it easier for people to visit each other and see how people in other places lived.

The railroads also helped Connecticut's *economy.* Farmers and manufacturers used the railroads to send their products to new markets.

Large amounts of money were needed to build the railroads. This helped the banking and insurance businesses grow.

Steam engines moved the trains. Soon people and goods were traveling faster than ever before.

Immigrants Build Connecticut

There were not enough American workers to build all the new roads, canals, and railroads. Companies spread the word to European countries that there were jobs in America. Many people left their homes and families to come to the United States.

People from Scotland and England had been coming to Connecticut for many years. In the early 1800s, people from other parts of Europe began to join them.

Industry Brings Change

Large groups of *immigrants* came from Germany and Ireland. These workers, farmers, and craftsmen helped to build our state and nation.

Irish Immigrants

In Ireland, many families were poor. They survived on potatoes, a crop that grew well there. One year a disease hit the potato plants. The potatoes rotted, and the people were starving.

Many of the Irish immigrants had been too poor to go to school in Ireland. When they arrived in America, they had to take jobs that did not require an education. Irish men worked in factories and helped build the roads, canals, and railroads that were so important to our young nation. They worked on the Enfield and Farmington Canals. They helped build the Hartford and New Haven Railroads.

Irish women cleaned and did laundry for other families. Children helped the adults. They gave their pennies to their parents to buy food or pay rent.

Because they took factory jobs, many Irish people settled in the cities. They started Catholic churches in those cities.

Immigrants are people who move to a new country to live.

Irish workers get ready to leave for America.

The Connecticut Adventure

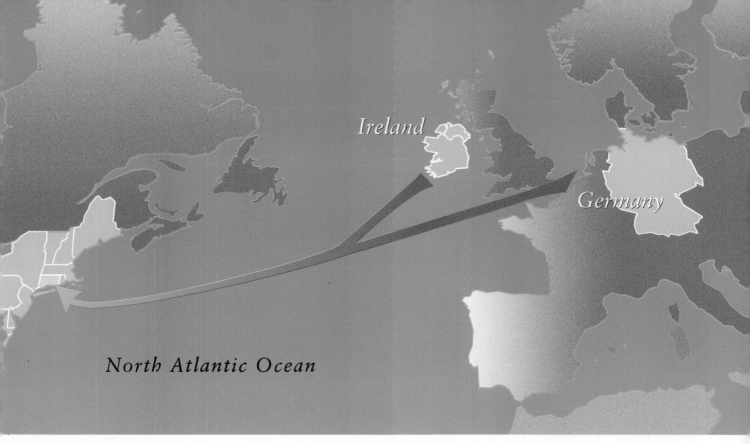

Ireland

Germany

North Atlantic Ocean

Immigrants from Ireland and Germany came to Connecticut.

German Immigrants

Many Germans lived in New Haven and Hartford. They worked as blacksmiths, machine workers, and skilled workers at the Colt Firearms Company. Colt brought Germans to Hartford to make furniture from the willow trees near his gun factory. Cheney Brothers, a silk company in Manchester, hired Germans as weavers and loom workers.

New Haven's German Jews became tailors, merchants, druggists, and restaurant owners. In Hartford, many opened clothing stores. Gerson Fox was the founder of G. Fox department stores.

German immigrants started their own churches and newspapers. Jews started synagogues in New Haven and Hartford.

Linking the past to the present

- **What is your favorite toy? Was it made by hand or mass produced by machines?**
- **Why do goods made in large quantities have a lower price than items that are made by hand, one at a time?**

These immigrants worked long hours in a shoe factory.

Women made cloth on huge machines.

Growth Brings Problems

So much production made our country rich and strong. It made many goods available at a low price. But there were prob lems, too.

Poor Working and Living Conditions

Often the men, women, and children in a family all worked for the factory owner. They lived in crowded apartments called *tenements*. The family paid rent to the factory owner. They bought what they needed at the company store.

The people worked from sunrise to sunset. The factories were dark and dangerous. Sometimes the machines injured workers. If a machine cut off a worker's hand, he was fired be cause he could no longer do his job.

For all this, the people were paid very low wages. Women and girls who spun cloth made about $2.58 a week. Men made a dollar more. Young children made less.

Children at Work

Children worked right along with men and women. Some mill owners set up night schools and Sunday schools for the children. It was hard for children to learn after working all day in the factory.

In 1842, a law cut down the hours that children could work each day. Children under fifteen could not work in factories until they had a certificate showing that they had gone to school for at least three months a year.

Children worked in factories. These children are stripping tobacco leaves.

A Time of Reform

Many people worked to reform, or change, society. They wanted to make life better for people. Thomas Gallaudet created a sign language for the deaf. He started the American School for the Deaf in West Hartford. It was the first free school for the deaf in America.

Mentally ill people had been treated very poorly. They were often locked up in cold, damp jail cells. Dr. Eli Todd wanted to change how they were treated. He started the Hartford Retreat. It cared for its patients with sympathy and kindness.

Some reformers wanted to do away with alcoholic drinks. They thought alcohol made people do bad things. They passed a law that made the sale of liquor illegal.

Women's groups tried to close the saloons in some cities. They gathered and prayed outside of the saloons.

Changes in Education

Henry Barnard fought to improve education. He started schools to train teachers. He became the first principal of a new teacher's college.

African American children were not allowed to attend school with the other children. Most black children did not go to school at all. Only Hartford and New Haven had separate schools for black students. Plans for an African American college in New Haven were turned down. However, more people were becoming aware that black people deserved an education. They started to speak out about freedom and equality.

What kinds of learning tools do you see in this one-room schoolhouse in Monroe?
(Photo by Jack McConnell)

The Connecticut Adventure

The Rights of African Americans

By 1820, most blacks in Connecticut were no longer slaves. They were free, but they were not considered equal to white people. They did not have many rights. For example, they were not allowed to vote. They lived mostly in poor sections of the cities. It was hard for blacks to get a good education and a good job.

Many black people organized societies to protect their freedom. Churches helped them come together. The first black church was the Temple Street Church in New Haven. The people were led by black ministers such as James W.C. Pennington of Hartford and Amos Beman of New Haven.

Some white people got together with free blacks to win more rights for African Americans. They were called abolitionists. An *abolitionist* is someone who wants to end, or abolish, slavery. Groups of abolitionists met in Connecticut as early as 1790. We will read more about abolitionists in the next chapter.

Women's Rights

During this time, women did not have many rights. They could not vote or own land. They could not go to college with men. When they got married, everything they had went to their husbands.

Many Connecticut women believed that they should have equal rights. The following women helped give other women more opportunities:

- **Emma Hart Willard** of Hartford founded the Emma Willard School for girls in New York.

- **Sarah Porter** founded Miss Porter's School in Farmington.

- **Catherine Beecher** and her sister Mary founded the Hartford Female Seminary.

- **Prudence Crandall** started a school for black girls called the Canterbury Female Boarding School.

- **Lydia Howard Sigourney** of Hartford wrote poetry. She became known as the "Sweet Singer of Hartford."

Connecticut Portrait

James W.C. Pennington
1807–1870

James Pennington was born a slave in Maryland. When he was twenty years old he escaped from slavery. He worked his way north by following the North Star.

In the North, James learned to read and write. He became a minister. He moved to New Haven, where he taught school and became a pastor at Temple Street Church.

Even though James lived as a free man in Connecticut, he was still legally a slave. Sometimes he had bad dreams about his owner hunting him down. Finally, he bought his freedom in Hartford for just one dollar.

James became an abolitionist leader. He turned one of his churches into a safe place for runaway slaves to stay. He raised money to help end slavery. He worked hard to change the conditions for black people in Connecticut.

Prudence Crandall
Our State Heroine

Prudence Crandall
(Painting by Carl Henry)

In the town of Canterbury, Prudence Crandall opened a school for young women. When she let Sarah Harris--a young black woman--into her school, the people of Canterbury were very angry.

Even though most people in Connecticut were against slavery, they did not accept people who were different from them. When Sarah Harris started going to the school, the white girls stopped going.

Prudence did not give up. She decided to make her school an academy only for black girls. With the help of a minister and some people who were strongly against slavery, she found twenty black students from around New England.

Prudence and her students faced hard times and even violence. She had to go to court two times. The school's well water was poisoned. After the building was attacked by a mob, Prudence had to close the school.

The wife of an Episcopal clergyman . . . told me that,

if I continued that colored girl in my school,

it could not [stay afloat]. I replied to her that it

might sink, then, for I should not turn her out.

—*Prudence Crandall*

What do you think?

- **What makes someone a hero?**
- **Who are some of your favorite heroes?**

The Connecticut Adventu

Prudence Crandall is remembered for her courage. She did what she believed was right, even though it was not popular. Many years later, in 1995, she became Connecticut's state heroine. A *heroine* is a woman who is admired for something she did.

PRUDENCE CRANDALL,

PRINCIPAL OF THE CANTERBURY, (CONN.) FEMALE

BOARDING SCHOOL.

RETURNS her most sincere thanks to those who have patronized her School, and would give information that on the first Monday of April next, her School will be opened for the reception of young Ladies and little Misses of color. The branches taught are as follows:— Reading, Writing, Arithmetic, English Grammar, Geography, History, Natural and Moral Philosophy, Chemistry, Astronomy, Drawing and Painting, Music on the Piano, together with the French language.

☞ The terms, including board, washing, and tuition, are $25 per quarter, one half paid in advance.

☞ Books and Stationary will be furnished on the most reasonable terms.

For information respecting the School, reference may be made to the following gentlemen, viz.—

ARTHUR TAPPAN, Esq.
Rev. PETER WILLIAMS,
Rev. THEODORE RAYMOND,
Rev. THEODORE WRIGHT, } N. YORK CITY.
Rev. SAMUEL C. CORNISH,
Rev. GEORGE BOURNE,
Rev. Mr. HAYBORN,

Mr. JAMES FORTEN, } PHILADELPHIA.
Mr. JOSEPH CASSEY,

Rev. S. J. MAY,—BROOKLYN, CT.
Rev. Mr. BEMAN,—MIDDLETOWN, CT.
Rev. S. S. JOCELYN,—NEW-HAVEN, CT.
Wm. LLOYD GARRISON } BOSTON, MASS.
ARNOLD BUFFUM,
GEORGE BENSON,—PROVIDENCE, R. I.

In 1833, Prudence printed this advertisement to get students for her school. She wanted to find "young Ladies and little Misses of color."

Activity

Looking at Advertisements

What can advertisements tell us about how the people of the past lived?

Look at this ad for carriages. What does it tell you about the carriages? Why might a customer want to know these things?

Compare this ad to a modern advertisement for a car. What does the modern ad tell you about the car? Why might a customer want to know this? Does the ad tell or show what is important to customers?

Activity

Studying a Chart

You've learned a lot of new things! How can you organize them in your head? Charts make it easier to organize things you have learned. Here is an example. This chart shows why industry was so successful in Connecticut.

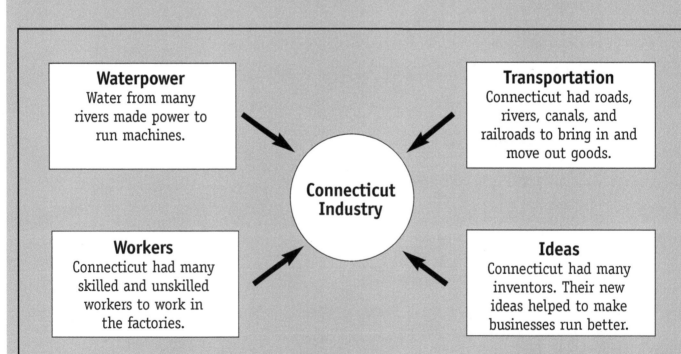

Waterpower
Water from many rivers made power to run machines.

Transportation
Connecticut had roads, rivers, canals, and railroads to bring in and move out goods.

Connecticut Industry

Workers
Connecticut had many skilled and unskilled workers to work in the factories.

Ideas
Connecticut had many inventors. Their new ideas helped to make businesses run better.

Listening to Folk Songs

Not everyone welcomed the railroads. Men who had made their living by driving wagons and carriages for people were now out of work. Here is a song they sang about how they felt:

The Wagoners' Curse on the Railroad

Come all ye bold wag'ners turn out man by man,
That's opposed to the railroad or any such plan;
'Tis once I made money by driving my team,
But the goods are now hauled on the railroad by steam.

May the devil get the fellow that invented the plan.
It'll ruin us poor wag'ners and every other man.
It spoils our plantations wherever it may cross,
And it ruins our markets, so we can't sell a hoss.

Come all ye bold wag'ners that have got good wives;
Go home to your farms and there spend your lives.
When your corn is all cribbed and your small grain is sowed,
You'll have nothing to do but curse the railroad.

Now it's your turn. Write a song about some change in your life. Use the words people use in everyday conversation. When you are finished, share it with your class.

Chapter 7 Review

1. What was the Industrial Revolution? How did it affect life in Connecticut?

2. List three goods that were made in Connecticut in the 1800s.

3. How did Eli Whitney help industry grow?

4. How did canals improve transportation?

5. List two kinds of jobs Irish immigrants had. List two jobs German immigrants had.

6. List three problems that came with the growing industries and cities.

7. How did people try to change things for the better? List two examples.

8. Why was Prudence Crandall important to Connecticut?

Geography Tie-In

The earliest immigrants to our state came from England, Scotland, Ireland, and Germany. Locate these countries on your classroom map. Use the map scale to figure out how many miles the immigrants had to travel to get to Connecticut.

The Civil War

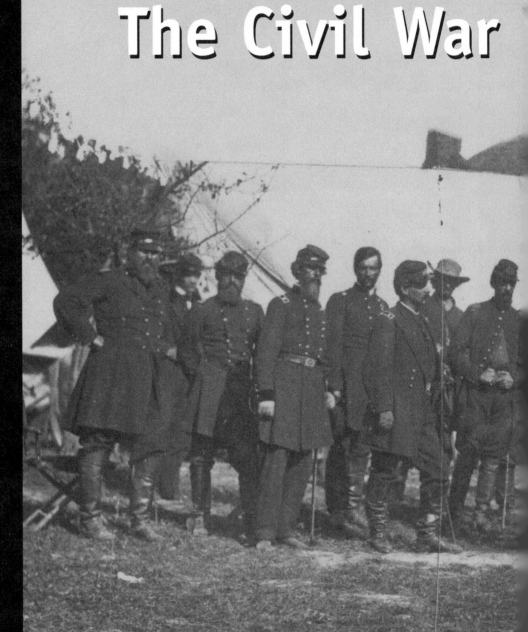

THE TIME
1830–1870

PEOPLE TO KNOW
Cinque
John Quincy Adams
Harriet Beecher Stowe
John Brown
Abraham Lincoln
John Wilkes Booth

PLACES TO LOCATE
New Haven
Litchfield
Hartford
Middletown
Bridgeport
Naugatuck Valley
Connecticut River
Long Island Sound
Kansas
Harpers Ferry, Virginia
Washington, D.C.
Africa
Cuba
Canada
Atlantic Ocean

Timeline of Events   1830   1835   1840

1839
Slaves aboard the
Amistad revolt and
are brought to
Connecticut.

Chapter 8

WORDS TO UNDERSTAND
arsenal
assassinate
bayonet
border state
civil war
Confederacy
emancipation
mutiny
overseer
plantation
rebellion
secede
segregation
Underground Railroad
Union

Connecticut sent soldiers to fight in the Civil War. President Abraham Lincoln visited the troops.

1850–1865 Some slaves escape to freedom on the Underground Railroad.

1859 John Brown leads a raid at Harpers Ferry, Virginia.

1863 Lincoln issues the Emancipation Proclamation.

1864 Lincoln is re-elected.

1870
The Fifteenth Amendment gives African American men the right to vote.

1850   1855   1860   1865   1870

1852
Harriet Beecher Stowe's book, *Uncle Tom's Cabin,* is published.

1861
Abraham Lincoln becomes president. A group of southern states leaves the Union.

1865
The Thirteenth Amendment ends slavery in the U.S. Lincoln is assassinated.

1861–1865
Civil War

1868
Segregation in Connecticut public schools is outlawed. The Fourteenth Amendment gives citizenship to African Americans.

131

A Nation Divided

By the middle of the 1800s, our country had grown and changed. Different parts of the country grew in different ways.

In the North, industry became very important. People built new cities. Some cities grew very large. The northern states outlawed slavery. Some people had small farms, but they could do most of the work themselves. Most of the powerful people worked in business and industry.

In the South, farming was still the most important part of the economy. Cotton was the most important crop. Slaves did a lot of the hard work. Many of the powerful people owned *plantations*. They were very large farms.

Because of all their differences, the North and the South wanted different things from the government. The North wanted it to help business and industry. The South wanted it to help agriculture.

Slavery

More and more, people in the North criticized Southerners for owning slaves. Most Northerners believed that slavery was wrong.

The Declaration of Independence said that "all men are created equal." But slaves were not considered equal to white people. They were thought of as property.

Many Southerners believed that they needed slaves to grow the cotton that brought wealth to the South. They did not want to change the system of slavery that had existed for hundreds of years.

Some of our great-great grandfathers and grandmothers were slaves. Some were slave owners. Some of our grandparents were not even in this country in the

The North

The South

(Drawing by Jon Burton)

The Connecticut Adventure

days of slavery. Today, we are neither slaves nor slave owners. But it is important for us to understand what slavery was like because it is a part of our history.

Linking the past to the present

In what ways can people today help to improve things that were unfair in the past?

Slaves at Work

Most slaves worked on plantations in the South. Men, women, and children over the age of six put seeds in the ground, took care of the plants, and harvested the crops. They worked for twelve or fourteen hours a day in the hot sun or in the rain.

Other slaves learned skilled crafts. They worked as carpenters, blacksmiths, and boot makers. Slaves also cooked, cleaned, and took care of children in the plantation owner's house.

Slaves worked in the fields from sunup to sundown. At night their backs ached from bending over all day. They were not paid for the hard work they did.

The Civil War

Slave Families

Like all people, every slave child had a mother and a father. Slaves had sisters and brothers, aunts and uncles, grandmothers and grandfathers. Often, family members lived near each other. But, at any time, an owner could sell a slave to someone who lived far away.

At slave auctions, where slaves were sold to the highest bidders, mothers were dragged from their children. Brothers and sisters were torn apart. Sometimes they never saw each other again. Even if everybody cried, it did no good.

Slaves were not allowed to control their own lives. They could not go to school at all. They could not choose their own jobs. They could not speak the thoughts that were on their minds.

> "My brothers and sisters were bid off first . . . while my mother . . . held me by the hand. Then I was offered. My mother pushed through the crowd to the spot where [her master] was standing. She fell at his knees, [begging] him . . . to buy her baby as well as herself."
>
> —*Josiah Henson*

CASH!

All persons that have SLAVES to dispose of, will do well by giving me a call, as I will give the

HIGHEST PRICE FOR

Men, Women, & CHILDREN.

Any person that wishes to sell, will call at Hill's tavern, or at Shannon Hill for me, and any information they want will be promptly attended to.

Thomas Griggs.

Charlestown, May 7, 1835.

PRINTED AT THE FREE PRESS OFFICE, CHARLESTOWN.

Advertisements of slaves for sale were seen in newspapers all over the South.

Punishments

If a slave did something the owner did not like, the owner might whip or beat the slave. Sometimes an owner with a lot of slaves hired an *overseer* to make sure the slaves did their work. The overseer gave out punishments so the owner did not have to do this unpleasant job himself.

Most white people did not like it when slave owners used cruel punishments. But, most of the time, no one stopped them.

What do you think?

Why is it important to remember the terrible, sad parts of history as well as the good parts?

Many Slaves Rebelled

It is no surprise that slaves did not like living under such cruel conditions. Some slaves rose up in *rebellion* against their owners. Many more ran away.

Some slaves did not want to risk the punishment they would get if they were caught planning a rebellion or trying to escape. Often they just decided not to work very hard. That was another way to rebel against slavery.

Mostly men ran away, but some women and children escaped to freedom.

Mutiny on the Amistad

In 1839, a group of Africans was kidnapped from their homes and families. They were chained together and forced into the bottom of a slave ship with hundreds of other slaves. It was dark and very crowded. There were no windows or bathrooms. Many people got sick and died on the ship.

After a long trip across the Atlantic Ocean to Cuba, some of the Africans were sold to Spanish planters. They boarded another ship called the *Amistad* bound for another part of Cuba.

These iron chains were found on the ship.

While at sea, the Africans wanted to know where they were going. But they did not speak the same language as the crew. An African man named Cinque decided to be their leader. He used sign language to ask the cook what was going to happen to them. The cook—making a joke of it—made signs that they would all be killed and eaten.

Cinque and the Africans took over the ship. This is called **mutiny**. In the fight, they killed the captain and the cook. Then they ordered the crew to turn around and sail back to Africa.

The crewmen headed to Africa by day, but each night they secretly tried to sail back to Cuba. After many days of zig-zagging through the ocean, they ended up in Long Island Sound. There the *Amistad* was spotted by an American ship.

A vessel was discovered off our coast on Wednesday under very mysterious circumstances. . . .
    —New York Morning Herald, August 24, 1839

The Africans were taken to the New Haven jail. Some people said they were murderers and should be returned to slavery. But the slave trade with Africa was against the law. Many people said that the Africans were victims who had a right to do what they did. They said the Africans should go free.

These blacks have created a greater excitement in Connecticut than any event . . . since the close of the last century. . . . The parsons preach about them, the men talk about them, the ladies give tea parties and discuss their . . . heroism [and] sufferings; . . .
    —New York Morning Herald, October 4, 1839

Abolitionists tried to help the Africans. The people of New Haven brought them clothing and food. They gave the Africans money so they could have a fair trial. Many of the Africans died in prison while waiting for the trials to end.

The case went all the way to the U.S. Supreme Court. Former President John Quincy Adams defended the Africans. He said they had a right to fight for their freedom. Adams won the case. Finally, the Africans were freed! Most of them went home to Africa.

Cinque
(Painting by Nathaniel Jocelyn, Courtesy of the New Haven Colony Historical Society)

What do you think?

If you were a young boy or girl on the *Amistad*, would you have wanted to follow Cinque and revolt? Why or why not?

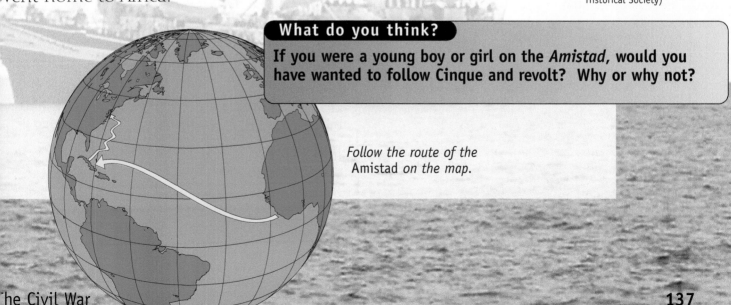

Follow the route of the Amistad on the map.

Working to End Slavery

Most people in Connecticut were against slavery. Many of them were abolitionists. Free black people and white abolitionists worked hard to end slavery. They did not want it to be legal anywhere in our country.

In addition to helping slaves, abolitionists helped blacks in the North. They gave them loans and money. They helped them start schools and churches to build stronger communities.

Here are the stories of two Connecticut abolitionists who tried to end slavery in two very different ways:

Harriet Beecher Stowe

Harriet Beecher Stowe was born in Litchfield. She grew up hating slavery. Her father, brothers, and uncles were abolitionists. She married a very religious abolitionist.

Harriet Beecher Stowe

When she traveled to different parts of the country, Harriet listened to the many stories of slaves who had run away. She wanted all Americans to know that slaves were people with real feelings. She used her imagination to weave these stories into a book called *Uncle Tom's Cabin*.

Uncle Tom's Cabin described the horrors of slavery. It told the story of a slave named Uncle Tom. He was a good man who tried to help all the other slaves he met. The book also told the story of the slave Eliza. She had a five-year-old son. She would not let her son be sold away from her. She carried him across an icy river to freedom.

Many Americans who read the book had great sympathy for the slaves. They realized that slaves had hopes and dreams like everyone else. They deserved to be free. *Uncle Tom's Cabin* became an instant bestseller.

Later in her life, Harriet moved to Hartford. She lived there for almost thirty years until she died. Her home is now a museum.

Read this advertisement for Uncle Tom's Cabin. *How many volumes had been sold?*

The Connecticut Adventure

John Brown

John Brown was born in Torrington. When he was five years old his family moved to Ohio. From a young age, John Brown hated slavery. He became one of the most famous abolitionists in America.

In the Kansas Territory, slavery was a hot issue. John Brown and his sons went there to help fight against it. After some abolitionists were killed, John and his sons wanted revenge. They killed a few of the men who wanted to keep slavery legal.

About a year later, John developed a plan. He wanted to free the slaves immediately—even if it meant using weapons and force. He organized a group of men in Virginia. One day the group seized the U.S. *arsenal* (a place where guns are made and stored) at Harpers Ferry. They took control of the town.

Brown and his men were soon surrounded by the local militia. A fight broke out, and some of the men were killed. John Brown was arrested. He was tried for treason and murder.

At the trial, Brown said he was trying to defend the slaves. He was found guilty and put to death by hanging. Many people agreed that John Brown had gone too far, but some abolitionists thought of him as a hero.

John Brown organized a group of men to help free the slaves.

John Brown is still remembered at Harpers Ferry.
(Photo by Tom Till)

The Underground Railroad

Slaves often traveled on the rivers to stay out of the way of people.

Free blacks and whites joined together to help slaves escape to the North. They set up a secret system called the Underground Railroad. The **Underground Railroad** was not really a railroad. It was a system of secret routes that slaves used to escape. It was not really underground either. "Underground" just means that it was hidden from most people.

The people who helped the runaways were called "conductors." They hid slaves in homes, barns, and churches as they moved north. These safe hiding places were called "stations." There were Underground Railroad stations all the way to Canada.

Many of the routes went through Connecticut. Slaves moved up the Connecticut River, then made their way to Canada. Francis Gillette's barn in Hartford was a station. In Plainville, a plaque marks the spot where the John Norton house used to be. John Norton offered a safe place for runaway slaves to hide.

The dots show where runaway slaves found safe places to stay as they traveled through Connecticut. With your finger, trace some of the routes they may have taken on their way north.

The Joshua Hempsted House in New London was a "station" on the Underground Railroad. Nancy Hempsted and her sisters were abolitionists. They ran a school for blacks and whites in their home.

Routes to Freedom

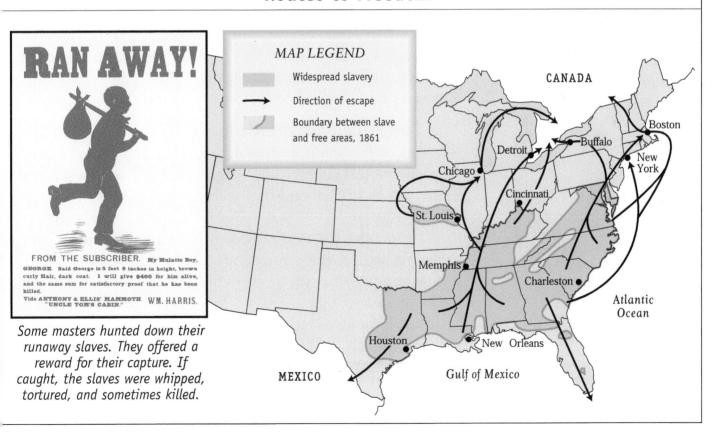

Some masters hunted down their runaway slaves. They offered a reward for their capture. If caught, the slaves were whipped, tortured, and sometimes killed.

Things Get Worse between the North and South

Americans argued about the issues that divided the North from the South. Congressmen and senators in Washington disagreed about everything from taxes to slavery.

Northerners said that people from the South were bad people because they owned slaves. Southerners said that northern industries made cloth from cotton grown by slaves. So, said the Southerners, the Northerners had no right to criticize.

Tempers grew hot. The more the abolitionists attacked slavery, the more determined the slave owners became. They said they didn't want Northerners telling them what to do.

Abraham Lincoln

The United States held an election for a new president in 1860. Four men were candidates. Abraham Lincoln, a lawyer from Illinois, was the winner.

Abraham Lincoln wanted the states to solve their problems peacefully together. He was also against slavery. During the campaign, Lincoln often said, "A house divided against itself cannot stand." This meant that the United States could no longer be half-slave and half-free.

The South Leaves the Union

Across the South, people decided that they did not want to be a part of this country any longer. One by one, the southern states *seceded*. They said they were no longer part of the United States.

The southern states formed their own government. They called themselves the Confederate States of America, or the *Confederacy*. When the Confederate states seceded, our country was split in two.

The northern states were called the *Union*. There were four slave states that did not leave the Union. They were called *border states*. Slavery was still legal in the border states.

Abraham Lincoln was president of the United States during the Civil War. He wanted all the states to stay together as one country.

Choosing Sides

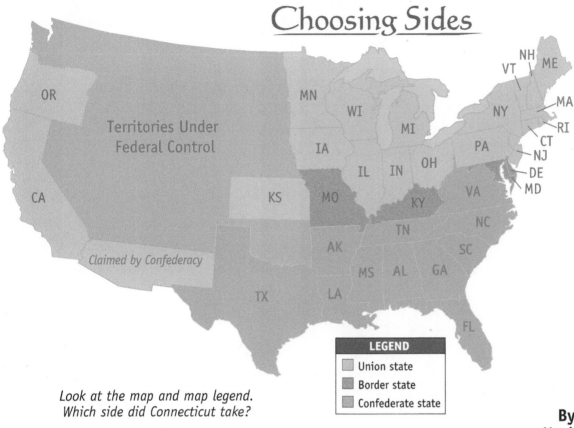

Territories Under
Federal Control

Claimed by Confederacy

OR
CA
MN
WI
IA
IL IN OH
MI
KS
MO
KY
AK
TN
MS AL GA
TX
LA
FL
VA
NC
SC
PA
NY
NH
VT ME
MA
RI
CT
NJ
DE
MD

LEGEND
Union state
Border state
Confederate state

*Look at the map and map legend.
Which side did Connecticut take?*

War Begins

President Lincoln said that states could not secede. He said that Americans would not be allowed to break up their country.

The Confederacy wanted to be on its own. Its men were armed and ready to fight. Soon, a *civil war* (a war between people in the same country) began.

What do you think?

- **What would it be like to live in a country where people went to war if they did not like the results of an election?**
- **What do Americans do when they are unhappy with election results?**

By this time, *Uncle Tom's Cabin* had become very popular. When President Lincoln met Harriet Beecher Stowe, he reached down to shake her hand. (He was over six feet tall.) He said jokingly, "So you're the little woman who wrote the book that started this great war!"

Connecticut in the Civil War

As soon as the war broke out, men in Connecticut volunteered to fight for the Union. After their three-month term was up, many men signed up again. Soon Connecticut had over 10,000 men in service.

Many of Connecticut's African Americans wanted to fight for the Union. They formed two black regiments. There was also an Irish regiment. Almost 8,000 Irish men from Connecticut served in the military.

As the war went on, President Lincoln called for more soldiers. Men from Connecticut served in the army, navy, and

People cheered for the Union soldiers as they left to fight.

marines. They fought in most of the important battles, including Bull Run and Gettysburg.

Factories in Connecticut supplied the army with cannons. The Collinsville Ax Company made *bayonets*. Textile mills made uniforms. Guns were made in Hartford, New Haven, and Middletown.

Carriage companies in New Haven made army wagons. Brass mills in the Naugatuck Valley made buttons for uniforms. The shipbuilding industry made ships for the navy. Mystic Seaport produced steamships.

Union soldier

A Soldier's Life

Many young men joined the army thinking the war would be exciting and short. They dreamed of being brave heroes. But usually the war was not like that. Soldiers spent most days sitting in camp, waiting for a battle. When the battles came, they were horrible.

An officer described what it was like to be at the Battle of Gettysburg:

> The smoke was so thick. So very thick was it that the sun seemed blotted out. One of the guns was directly behind me . . . and I could not only see and smell the thick cloud of burning powder, but could taste it also. I lay with my arm thrown over Eddy Hart and so hot was it that the drops of perspiration falling from my face made mud of the dusty soil on which we were stretched.
>
> —History of the Fourth Regiment by Charles D. Page

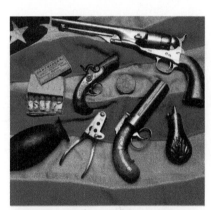

These are some of the weapons used by Union and Confederate soldiers.

Often the armies were not able to give the soldiers the things they needed. Sometimes soldiers did not have shoes. Sometimes they ran out of food. If this happened, the soldiers often raided homes and farms to steal what they needed.

Diseases killed a lot of soldiers. The water supply was often dirty. Human waste lay all around. Men got sick and died. In some camps, more men died of disease than from battle.

Young Boys Go to War

Most soldiers were at least eighteen years old, but some younger boys went to war. In the North, boys as young as nine years old played drums for the troops. Other boys went to visit their fathers and stayed on to fight. Many boys lied about their ages so they could go to the battlefield.

This boy joined the army when he was ten years old. He was the youngest soldier in the Union army.

This young boy was a slave who became a drummer for the Union army.

The Connecticut Adventu

Young boys soon learned that being in the army meant a lot more marching than fighting. They marched for miles and miles. They marched through mud and dust, in the rain, in the heat, and in the cold. They slept in tents or just out on the cold, wet ground. Often they had very little to eat.

Many of the boys became homesick and scared. The battles were terrible. The boys saw their friends wounded or killed.

Elisha Stockwell described what he was feeling in the middle of a battle:

> *As we lay there and the shells were flying over us, my thoughts went back to my home, and I thought what a foolish boy I was to run away and get into such a mess as I was in.*

After the war, the government changed its rules. The Civil War was the last time so many young boys fought for our country.

Women and the War Effort

Women wanted to help win the war. They volunteered to care for the wounded soldiers. They knitted socks and sewed bandages. They raised money to send to the soldiers. They helped the families whose sons had volunteered to fight. A few women served as spies or dressed up as boys and joined the army.

In Norwich, women made uniforms for the men from their town. New Haven women made 500 uniforms. In East Hartford, women stuffed mattresses with straw and sewed uniforms. The Ladies' Soldiers Relief Society of Bridgeport sent vegetables and supplies to the soldiers.

The Emancipation Proclamation

Finally, President Lincoln decided that slavery must be abolished. In the middle of the war, he issued the *Emancipation* Proclamation. All slaves in the Confederacy were now free. He did not free slaves in the border states because he didn't want to upset states that had been loyal to the Union.

For slaves in the South it was a day of great rejoicing. They sang, "Thank God, I'm free at last!"

"There is a piece in the paper this morning saying that the 2nd regiment went off most shamefully equipped. Is it so? . . . Whatever it is they shall have it immediately if you will but let the New Haven Ladies know through me. Our interest in these men is not to be shown in mere words. These men must have clothes, proper knapsacks, canteens, . . . blankets . . ."

—*Harriet Terry to Colonel Alfred Terry*

President Lincoln was shot while sitting with his wife, Mary, in a private theater box. The man who shot Lincoln jumped down to the stage and broke his leg, but ran out a back door and rode away on a horse.

The War Comes to an End

For four long years, Americans fought one another. Finally, the war ended. The Confederacy lost the war. It came back as part of the United States. The war had shown everyone that Americans could not split their country in two.

The Loss of a Leader

In many Connecticut towns, people celebrated with parades and speeches. But joy quickly turned to sorrow. Only days after the war ended, President Lincoln was *assassinated.*

A man named John Wilkes Booth shot President Lincoln while he was watching a play at Ford's Theater in Washington, D.C. The next morning the president was dead. Both black and white Americans were very sad to lose such a great leader.

Connecticut after the War

Soon after the war, the Thirteenth Amendment was added to the U.S. Constitution. It abolished slavery forever. African Americans in every state celebrated the end of slavery. In

Connecticut, just a few years later, a law was passed that said black children no longer had to go to separate schools. *Segregation* in the public schools would be against the law.

The Freedman's Bureau, a national group, helped former slaves. It built schools and gave food, shelter, and medicine to people who were in need.

African Americans helped themselves, too. They opened schools, often in church buildings. People with homes took in the homeless. Others fed the hungry until they could find work. It was a very difficult time.

Voting Rights

Across the country, African Americans said they should be allowed to vote. Some whites agreed. When the Fifteenth Amendment to the U.S. Constitution became a law, African Americans gained the right to vote everywhere in the country. Only black men won the right to vote. No women of any race were allowed to vote.

This picture was taken after the war had ended. There was no more slavery, and black men had the right to vote. This family posed in front of the house where John Brown had lived in Torrington.

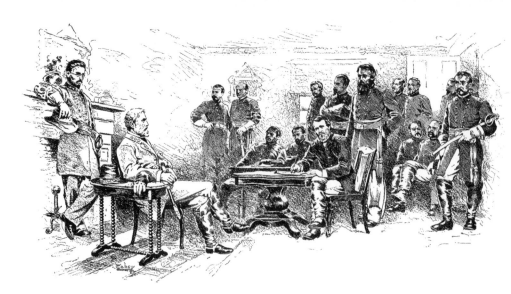

Confederate General Robert E. Lee surrendered to Union General Ulysses S. Grant.

Activity

Cause and Effect

When we enter a dark room and turn on the light switch, the room is filled with light. This is called cause and effect. The cause is flipping the light switch. The effect is that the room is filled with light. Life is filled with cause-and-effect relationships. Events in history also have causes and effects.

CAUSE: Something that happened first and caused something else to happen.
EFFECT: What happened as a result of the cause.

Look at each pair of sentences below. On a separate piece of paper, write "C" for the cause and "E" for the effect.

EXAMPLE:
C   Abraham Lincoln issued the Emancipation Proclamation.
E   Slaves were freed.

1. ____ Farmers in the South planted huge crops of cotton and tobacco.
   ____ They needed lots of field workers.

2. ____ Some slaves made it to freedom.
   ____ Brave people risked their lives to escape from slavery.

3. ____ A slave girl was punished by the master.
   ____ A slave girl was caught learning to read.

4. ____ Abraham Lincoln loved to read books and newspapers.
   ____ Lincoln could talk about many different subjects.

5. ____ The southern states left the Union.
   ____ Lincoln was elected president.

Activity

Songs Record History

Did you ever think of songs as a way of recording history? Before radio, television, and movies were invented, people entertained themselves by getting together to sing songs. Many songs were about politics. People sang them at political rallies. The slaves sang songs, too. Some of these songs talked about hard times, freedom, and the Underground Railroad.

In this song, the people talk about following the Big Dipper in the night sky on their journey north. They called the Big Dipper the "drinking gourd."

The river bank will make a very good road.
The dead trees will show the way.
Left foot, peg foot, travelin' on!

Follow the drinkin' gourd!
Follow the drinkin' gourd!
Follow the drinkin' gourd!

Your library might have songbooks that have old songs. Make it a class project to see how many songs you can find and how many you can learn to sing!

Chapter 8 Review

1. In what ways were the North and South different?
2. Was Connecticut a free state or a slave state?
3. Name two famous abolitionists from Connecticut.
4. What did the book *Uncle Tom's Cabin* have to do with the Civil War?
5. What was the Underground Railroad?
6. Who was president of the United States during the Civil War?
7. When the southern states left the Union, what did they call themselves?
8. What contributions did Connecticut make during the Civil War?
9. What terrible event happened just after the Civil War ended?
10. Which amendment to the U.S. Constitution gave African Americans the right to vote?

Geography Tie-In

Look at the map of Underground Railroad stops in Connecticut on page 141. Do you live near one of the Underground Railroad sites? If you do, check to see if you can visit.

THE TIME
1870–1920

PEOPLE TO KNOW
Charles Storrs
Augustus Storrs
P.T. Barnum
Mark Twain
Frederick Law Olmstead
William Gray
Isabella Beecher Hooker
Katharine Houghton
    Hepburn
Woodrow Wilson

PLACES TO LOCATE
New Haven
Bridgeport
Waterbury
Hartford
Taftville
Danbury
Thames River
Ellis Island
England
France
Russia
Germany
Austria
Turkey
Mississippi River

Into a New Century

1871
P.T. Barnum starts
"The Greatest
Show on Earth."

1874–1891
Mark Twain lives in
Connecticut, writing his
most famous books.

1879
Hartford becomes
the state capital.

Timeline of Events 1870 1875 1880 1

1870
African Americans
win the right to
vote.

1876
Alexander Graham Bell
invents the telephone.

1875
Taftville Cotton
Mill Strike

1881
Storrs Agricultural College
(now the University of
Connecticut) is started.

Chapter 9

WORDS TO UNDERSTAND
century
ethnic group
generator
middle-class
labor union
politics
Progressive
reliable
steerage
strike
suffrage
symbol
veteran

These girls are eating their lunches at school in the early 1900s. Does their classroom look like yours? Do their lunch pails look like yours? How are their clothes different from your classmates'?

1886
dren under thirteen
o longer allowed to
ork in factories.

1893
The first gasoline-powered
automobiles are invented.

1914–1918
World War I

The U.S. enters
the war in 1917.

1890   1895   1910   1915   1920

1880–1910
es of immigrants come to Connecticut.

A century is 100 years.

A New America

People often look forward to the beginning of a new *century.* They hope it will be a fresh start. That's how many people in Connecticut looked at the year 1900. It was the first year of the twentieth century. They could fix man of the things they wanted to change.

Changes on the Farm

After the Civil War, farming changed in Connecticut. Farming became more of a business. New machines and ideas helped farmers produce more. There were fewer farms, but farmers could grow more on the land they had.

These women worked in a tobacco barn. Their job was to sort the tobacco leaves and get them ready to be dried. Workers hung the leaves to dry in a shed.

(Photo of shed by Kindra Clineff)

Out in the western states, farmers had lots of land. They could produce more wheat and meat. They could use trains to move these products to eastern states.

Connecticut farmers could not compete with the western farmers. Instead, they sold the crops that would spoil if they had to be moved long distances by train. They sold fruits, vegetables, and dairy products such as fresh milk and cheese.

Tobacco grew well in the Connecticut River Valley. More and more farmers were growing tobacco leaves and drying them in their sheds. The dried leaves were sold and used to make cigars. By 1920, tobacco was Connecticut's most valuable crop.

Changes in the Factory

As the new century began, most people lived in cities, such as New Haven or Bridgeport. Workers made a lot of wool and silk textiles. They also produced goods made from brass, iron, gold, and silver.

Before the Civil War, Connecticut's mills were built next to rivers and waterfalls. The moving water turned wheels that moved parts in machines. As industry grew, more machines needed even more power than water could supply. Where would the power come from?

The answer was steam. Steam could make motors run. It could make machine parts move.

In order to create steam power, the people needed to heat water. They burned large amounts of coal. States with large supplies of coal shipped it to Connecticut's ports. Then the coal was moved inland by train.

Trains were important for bringing raw materials to the factories. They were also important for taking the goods to markets in far-away places. Many companies started to build more railroads. New Haven, Bridgeport, Waterbury, and Hartford became the state's leading industrial cities.

Charles and Augustus Storrs started an agricultural school. Storrs Agricultural College grew into the University of Connecticut.

Into a New Century

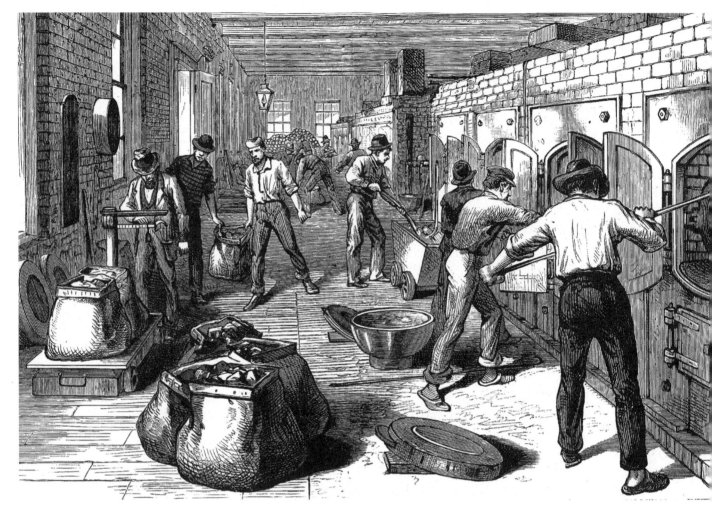

Burning coal made it possible to run factories in Connecticut.

Our state was a leader in making sewing machines.

Trains were not the only kind of transportation that used steam power. Steam engines were used to power boats, too. Steamboats brought goods and people to new places. They were faster than canal boats and sailing ships.

It was exciting to watch a steamboat come in to dock. Before the boat came into view you could hear a loud whistle. The pilot blew the whistle to announce the boat's arrival. Soon, just over the trees, you could see smoke and steam coming from the tall smokestacks. Then the ship pulled up to the shore.

Ropes were thrown to workers on the dock. Crew members shouted to one another. They swung large wooden ramps out from the boat so the passengers could walk to the shore. Everyone on the shore waited to meet the passengers or pick up their goods.

The Connecticut Adventure

People who lived near a river or Long Island Sound could ride on a steamboat in the summer.

A New State Capital

Since colonial days, Connecticut had had two capital cities—New Haven and Hartford. The state government met every other year in each city.

As time went by, the state government had more to do. Both statehouses needed repairs. The government decided to choose one city to be the state capital.

Both cities wanted to be the capital city. The people of Hartford said they had the best location. They offered money to build a new capitol building. The people of New Haven said they had more people and more wealth.

The state took a vote, and Hartford was the winner. The old statehouse in New Haven was torn down and a new capitol building was built in Hartford.

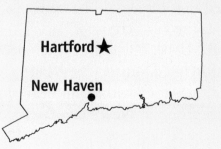

(Photo by Kindra Clineff)

An Albanian farmer

A Hungarian woman

A Russian immigrant

New Immigrants

With all the new industries and growing cities, there were lots of jobs. People from other countries came to take these jobs. They came from Japan, China, Mexico, the West Indies, and Canada. However, most of the immigrants who came to Connecticut during this time were from Europe. They came from England, Ireland, and Germany, as they had for many years. A new wave of immigrants came from other places in Europe such as Italy, Greece, Poland, and Russia. Like the earlier immigrants, most were very poor.

Immigrants looked to America as a "land of opportunity." They hoped they would find freedom here. They hoped they would find good jobs, decent homes, and enough to eat. They hoped that life would be better for their children here than it was in the "old country."

By 1910, one out of three people in the state had been born in a foreign country. An *ethnic group* is a group of people who share the same culture and traditions. Italians were the largest ethnic group in New Haven. Today, the area around Wooster Street in New Haven is called "Little Italy."

Some people say that pizza was invented in New Haven. Today, the city is known for its great pizza.

Journey to America

Many of the immigrants who came to America could only afford the least expensive steamship ticket. This was a *steerage* ticket. It let a person stay at the bottom of the ship, next to the engine room. It was very hot and noisy there. The food was often terrible, and the water was filthy. There was very little fresh air. Many people got sick.

Most of the new immigrants landed at Ellis Island in New York Harbor. As their ship got closer, they could see the Statue of Liberty. Many of them cried tears of joy when they first saw this *symbol* of hope and freedom.

At Ellis Island the immigrants had to stand in line while people wrote down their names and doctors gave them check-ups. Sick immigrants had to stay there until they got better. Some were even sent back to their homeland. Those who passed the exam could take a train to Bridgeport or New Haven.

"[There were] six of us kids . . . after two weeks and a bit seasick we unloaded . . . and we got an eye exam. Some man came along. He gave us a box of food. . . . In the box there was a banana. We didn't know how to eat it. We'd never seen bananas. Finally somebody realized that and showed us."
—Nicholas Gerros, Greece

Most immigrants brought only the few things they could carry.

From the Old World to the New World

Norway · Sweden · Finland · Russia · Denmark · England · Poland · Ireland · Germany · Italy · Greece · Canada · China · Japan · United States · Mexico · West Indies

Fitting In

Most immigrants were so poor that they had to live in the worst parts of the cities. They often settled in ethnic neighborhoods. There they could speak the language of their home country. They could eat the foods they were familiar with.

Churches held festivals. Some groups started newspapers and social clubs. The Sons of Italy, the Sons of Norway, the Knights of Columbus, and others helped people in times of need.

Not everyone treated the new immigrants well. Their languages and names seemed strange and were hard to say. They were given the lowest paying jobs.

Some of the old Yankees did not like so many Catholics moving in. They tried to keep Catholics out of *politics* and government. But the immigrants didn't give up. By 1900, Irish Catholics were winning elections in Connecticut.

Immigrants Help Connecticut Grow

Where They Came From	Where They Settled	Where They Worked
Ireland	Hartford, New Haven, Waterbury, Bridgeport	factories, railroads, schools, churches, police force, politics
Germany	Hartford, New Haven	factories, mechanic shops, construction jobs
Italy	Hartford, New Haven, Waterbury	factories, railroads, restaurants, barbershops, hotels
Eastern Europe (Jews)	Hartford, New Haven, Colchester, Lebanon, Chesterfield, Norwich	factories, bakeries, grocery stores, shoemaker shops, tailor shops, carpenter shops, farms
Poland	Hartford, New Haven, Waterbury, Bridgeport, New Britain	factories, farms
Greece, Hungary, Lithuania	Hartford, New Haven, Bridgeport	factories, restaurants

These Armenian immigrants went to school to learn English.

People Come from the South

Life in the South was very hard after the Civil War. Many former slaves and their families moved into the northern states.

Many African Americans came to Connecticut's growing cities. They hoped to find work in the booming factories or on the railroads.

Unsafe Places to Work

Immigrants and other people worked long hard hours. For all their work, they were paid very low wages. Women and children had to go to work so there would be enough money for food and rent.

The factories were hot in the summer and cold in the winter. They were noisy with the clatter of machines. They could be dangerous, too. If a machine hurt a worker, the worker could be fired. The company did not pay people who could not work.

Workers sometimes went on strike. A *strike* is when people refuse to work until the company gives them better pay and better working conditions. Sometimes the strikes led to violence. Angry workers destroyed company property. Policemen and workers fought each other.

African American children and their parents moved to Connecticut from the South.

Into a New Century

In cities by the water, women canned oysters. It was a dangerous job because they had to use sharp knives to open the shells.

In some cases, a strike did not help the workers. When workers at the Taftville Cotton Mill went on strike, the owners just hired other workers. The company owned the apartments where the workers lived, so it kicked the strikers and their families out of their homes.

Labor Unions

Workers got together to help make things better. They formed *labor unions*. The unions demanded higher pay and safe working conditions. Union leaders talked to government leaders and helped convince them to make laws that made factories safer places to work.

Inventions

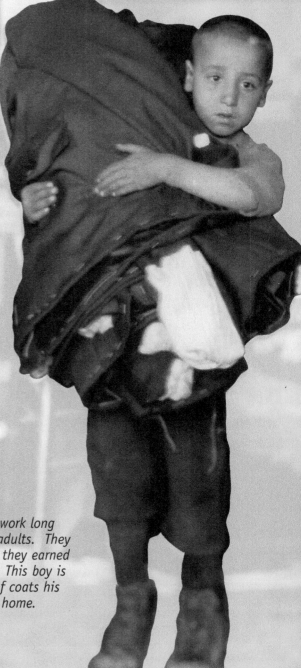

Children had to work long hours, just like adults. They gave the money they earned to their parents. This boy is carrying a pile of coats his family sewed at home.

Make Life Easier

Many things that we take for granted today did not exist 100 years ago. People did not have televisions and computers. Most did not have cars or telephones. If you could travel back in time—let's say to 1870—you would find that your life would be very different.

Electricity

In 1870, if you wanted to cook food or heat your house, you had to fill a stove with coal or wood, then light a fire. Today you turn a knob to get gas or electric heat.

To get light in 1870, you filled a lamp with kerosene and trimmed the wick every day. Today you flip a switch and your lights come on.

Electric generators were one of the most important new inventions. *Generators* are machines that make electricity. They changed the way people worked, played, and lived. Streets and homes were lit with electric lights for the first time. New machines that used electricity were invented. There were electric washing machines, irons, stoves, re-frigerators, and vacuum cleaners. Streetcars no longer had to be pulled by horses. They could run on electric wires.

Before electricity was used, women used hand-powered washing machines.

The Telephone

In 1870, if you wanted to talk to people across town, you had to write them a letter or go to see them.

Alexander Graham Bell's new invention—the telephone—made it easier for people to communicate. Soon people in Connecticut were making calls from town to town.

Over time, Bell's invention led to many other dis-coveries. Today, you can pick up the telephone and talk to people around the world. Your computer can use your phone line to send e-mail anywhere in the world!

The first machine to make lollipops was used in New Haven in 1908.

The first bicycle factory was started in Hartford in 1877.

William Gray of Hartford invented the coin-operated telephone and the baseball chest protector for catchers.

New Ways to Get Around

Cities grew so large that it was no longer possible to walk from one end to the other. People rode open buses pulled by horses. Once a city had electricity, the buses were replaced with "horseless carriages" or trolleys. Trolleys got their power from electric wires.

The first automobiles were built in the late 1800s. Wealthy people began to buy them. At first, people used cars mainly for fun. They were not very *reliable.* Because roads were not paved,

People often made fun of the early cars. When they saw a car in trouble, they yelled, "Get a horse!"

The Connecticut Adventure

cars got stuck in the mud all the time. There were no gas stations, so people had to fill up before they left home.

Time for Fun

Sometimes families took a trolley car to an amusement park. They went to Saven Rock and Lake Compounce. They stayed at the Griswold Inn or watched a show at the Goodspeed Opera House.

There were town fairs, where people hoped to win a blue ribbon for baked or canned foods, crafts, or prize animals. People danced and listened to bands. The Danbury Fair was the largest town fair.

Every summer the Yale-Harvard rowing races on the Thames River brought thousands of visitors. People rode on trains that ran along both sides of the river, following the racers.

People went on picnics, just like we do today.

Connecticut Portrait

P.T. Barnum
1810–1891

Have you ever been to the circus? A man from Connecticut started America's most famous circus. His name was Phineas Taylor Barnum.

P.T. Barnum was born in Bethel. He became a showman and entertainer in New York. He decided to start a circus and museum that could travel from town to town. He called it "The Greatest Show on Earth."

People who went to the show got to see lots of animals, including a huge elephant named Jumbo. They wandered through the museum filled with interesting people and sights.

Soon P.T. Barnum became partners with another showman named James Bailey. They created the Barnum & Bailey Circus. It became famous across America and all around the world.

P.T. Barnum also served in Connecticut's legislature and as mayor of Bridgeport.

Mark Twain

One of the most popular authors during this time was Mark Twain. His real name was Samuel Langhorne Clemens.

Samuel Clemens grew up in Missouri, near the Mississippi River. He loved the river so much that he became a steamboat pilot. The call of "mark twain!" could be heard on the river when pilots were testing how deep the water was. "Twain" meant two measurements deep. Clemens used the nickname Mark Twain to sign a funny letter. He liked it, so the name stuck.

Twain and his family moved to Hartford when he was thirty-nine. He said Hartford was a "vision of refreshing green." He lived there for almost twenty years.

Twain's home was in an area called Nook Farm. Other writers, such as Harriet Beecher Stowe, lived in Nook Farm. There Twain wrote some of his most famous books, including *The Adventures of Tom Sawyer* and *The Adventures of Huckleberry Finn*.

> *I made two mile and a half, and then struck out . . . towards the middle of the river, because pretty soon I would be passing the ferry landing and people might see me and hail me. I got out amongst the drift-wood and then laid down in the bottom of the canoe and let her float. I laid there and had a good rest . . . looking away into the sky, not a cloud in it. They sky looks ever so deep when you lay down on your back in the moonshine; I never knowed it before.*

> *—The Adventures of Huckleberry Finn*

Mark Twain's stories are funny and full of adventure. They often criticized slavery and other bad things in our society. Today, Mark Twain is thought of as one of the best American writers.

Hartford

Samuel
Clemens

*What kinds of things
can you see in
Mark Twain's study?*
(Photo by Jack McConnell)

*Mark Twain lived in this house with his wife and three daughters. It had Hartford's first
telephone and a fountain that ran all winter long. Twain said the house had a
"heart, and a soul, and eyes to see us with."*
(Photo by Jack McConnell)

Into a New Century

The Rich and the Poor

Rich families and poor families lived very differently. A few people made large fortunes in business and industry. They were the first to have running water, electricity, and cars.

There were more poor people than rich people. In cities, poor families often lived in tenements that had no running water or inside bathrooms. They used an outhouse and an outside well or pump for water. When they did get running water, several families often shared a bathroom and a kitchen.

A lot of families were neither rich nor poor. They had homes and enough to eat, but not much else. Most children of these *middle-class* families went to school.

The families in this building shared one water faucet in the hall.

Entered according to Act of Congress, in the year 1880, by LEVY BROS., Madison, Ind., at the office of the Librarian of Congress at Washington.

RECORD
OF THE STANDING OF

Ida Hindman   Grade *1*

For the month ending   *Sept. 30*   18*81*.

	Deportment	95
A	Spelling	100
B	Reading	1
C	Arithmetic	100
D	Penmanship	
E	Geography	
F	Grammar	93
G	Composition	
H	Declamation	
I	History	100
J	Physiology	100
K	*Algebra*	78
L		

AVERAGE,   *95+*

Number Times Tardy

Number Times Absent

D. H. Swain   Teacher.

} Parents.

This report card was made for first-grader Ida Hindman. What subjects was she graded on? How does this compare to your report cards today?

Working to Make Things Better

The people faced many new problems. The cities had grown quickly. They were crowded and dirty. There were not enough policemen or firemen. The drinking water was dirty. No one came to pick up the garbage. The skies were filled with black smoke from the factories.

Many men and women tried to solve these problems. They wanted to make life better for everyone. They wanted our country to make good progress. That's why they were called *Progressives.*

One way we can change things is by electing good leaders. The people who make our laws are very important. They can make a real difference in how we live. In the early 1900s, a lot of Progressives won elections. Then they were able to make laws and clean up cities.

Progressives passed laws that said there had to be safety inspections in factories. They made companies give their workers better pay. They passed laws saying that all children had to go to school. This got children out of dangerous factories. An education also meant that children would be able to get better jobs when they grew up.

Cities started to pay workers to collect garbage. This kept the streets cleaner.

Linking the past to the present

What problems in your city or town need to be fixed? What things are better now than they used to be?

The Power of Voting

By this time, African Americans had been given the right to vote. Black men could elect leaders who would help look out for the needs of the people in their communities.

Connecticut Portrait

Frederick Law Olmstead
1822–1903

As the cities grew, people worried that there would be no open spaces left. They began to set aside large areas of land with trees, lakes, and nice grassy places for picnics.

Frederick Law Olmstead designed parks. Olmstead designed about eighty parks in all. One of his projects was the park system in his hometown of Hartford.

Olmstead became famous for his parks. He won a contest to create Central Park in New York City. He also designed the grounds around the U.S. Capitol in Washington, D.C.

Next time you go to a park, remember Frederick Law Olmstead and how he helped make our cities more beautiful!

These women spread the word that they should be able to vote.

Many people who had been born in other countries became American citizens. Then they could vote. Soon Irish, Italian, and Polish immigrants were helping to make our laws.

Most Progressives wanted women to be able to vote, too. But some men did not want women to be in politics. They thought women did not know enough to vote.

Connecticut women fought hard to get the right to vote. They held meetings and went to women's rights meetings all over the state and country. They marched in parades and hung flyers around town.

Isabella Beecher Hooker started a group called the Connecticut Woman Suffrage Association (CWSA). *Suffrage* is another word for the right to vote. The CWSA wrote letters, held meetings, gathered signatures, and talked to government leaders to try to get more rights for women.

Another Connecticut woman who worked hard to get women the vote was Katharine Houghton Hepburn. Her daughter, also named Katharine Hepburn, became a famous movie star.

The World Goes to War

Fast steamships, telephones, and radios helped the people of Connecticut connect with people from faraway places. For better or for worse, Connecticut was drawn into events that were happening all around the world.

A terrible war broke out in Europe in 1914. The countries in Europe took sides. England, France, Russia, and Italy joined together and supported each other. They fought against Germany, Austria, Turkey, and some other countries.

President Woodrow Wilson wanted to keep the United States out of the war. But after German submarines started sinking American ships, the United States joined the war. Thousands of soldiers from Connecticut went off to fight.

Connecticut in World War I

Everyone at home tried to help in the war effort. Families planted "victory gardens" to help grow more food. They turned their lights off early to save fuel. Women's clubs made bandages for wounded soldiers.

Children helped adults raise food through the Junior Food Army and the Connecticut Canning Corps. Students older than fourteen were allowed to volunteer for farm work. Everyone saved food so there would be more to send to the soldiers. They stopped eating meat on Tuesdays and wheat on Wednesdays.

Factories were busy making guns, tanks, ships, and other goods for the war. Remington Arms and Ammunition, Remington Union Metallic, Winchester Repeating Arms, Marlin Rockwell, and Colt's Firearms made most of the goods. Cheney Brothers of Manchester made silk for parachutes. Danbury hat factories made hats to go with army uniforms.

Some people moved into the cities to work in war industries. More and more African Americans from southern states came to Connecticut to get better jobs.

Posters were put up all over Connecticut. They asked people to support the war.

People called it the Great War. We now call it World War I.

Girl Scouts collected peach pits. The pits were turned into charcoal. Charcoal was used in gas masks to filter out poisonous gases.

The War Ends

Peace came when Germany surrendered. The countries signed a peace treaty on November 11, 1918. The news that the war was over arrived by telegraph.

In Connecticut and across the nation, everyone celebrated. Towns held parades to honor the soldiers. The troops marched through the streets as the people cheered. November 11 is now celebrated as Veterans' Day. A *veteran* is a person who served in the armed forces.

Linking the past to the present

Marcus Holcomb was governor of Connecticut during World War I. He was a "war governor" just as Jonathan Trumbull had been during the Revolutionary War. Who is our governor today?

The Connecticut Adventure

Activity

Studying Your Family History

Where did your ancestors come from? It's fun to trace your family back as far as you can go. Make a family tree. Write your name at the bottom of the trunk. See if you can find the names of some of your ancestors and when they first came to Connecticut.

Great Grandmother
Great Grandfather
Great Grandmother
Great Grandmother
Great Grandfather
Great Grandfather
Great Grandmother
Great Grandfather
Grandmother
Grandfather
Grandfather
Grandmother
Father
Mother
Self
OUR FAMILY TREE

Chapter 9 Review

1. What kinds of things did farmers produce to sell?

2. What natural resources did Connecticut factories use to get steam power for machines?

3. What city finally became the only capital of Connecticut?

4. List three reasons why immigrants came to America.

5. What jobs did immigrants do in Connecticut?

6. What were some problems that immigrants faced?

7. How did Connecticut help the country during World War I?

8. What holiday celebrates the end of World War I?

Geography Tie-In

1. On a map of the world, find the countries immigrants came from. What ocean(s) did they have to cross?

2. On a map of Connecticut, find the cities and towns where immigrants settled.

Chapter 10

THE TIME
1920–1945

PEOPLE TO KNOW
Katharine Hepburn
Marian Anderson
President Franklin
   Roosevelt
Adolf Hitler

PLACES TO LOCATE
New Fairfield
Bridgeport
Hartford
Branford
Stonington
Connecticut River
New York City
Harlem, New York
Pearl Harbor, Hawaii
Germany
Japan
China
Italy
France
Russia

Timeline of Events

1920
Women win the
right to vote.

1919–1933
Prohibition: Alcohol is
banned in the United States.

1922
WDRC starts a radio
broadcast from New Haven.

1920s
The Roaring
Twenties

1929
The stock
market crashes.

1920   1925

Chapter

10

Good Times and Bad Times

WORDS TO UNDERSTAND
ally
atomic bomb
concentration camp
conquer
depression
dictator
discrimination
Holocaust
independent
prejudice
prohibit
ration
renaissance
stock

After training in the United States, soldiers went to Europe to fight in World War II.

1936
The Connecticut
River floods.

1939–1945
World War II

1935

1940

1945

1938
A powerful hurricane
hits Connecticut.

1941
December 7
The Japanese bomb
Pearl Harbor, Hawaii.
The U.S. enters
World War II.

1930s
The Great Depression

The Roaring Twenties

Soon after World War I ended, new industries created new jobs. People could buy new products like radios and telephones. Rural families got electric power for the first time. They could keep food in a refrigerator. They could put away the gas lamps.

People wanted to forget about the war and just have fun. They went to sporting events and cheered for their heroes. There were all-night dance contests to see who could dance the longest. Couples danced a new dance called the Charleston. For the first time in America, women cut their hair short and wore shorter dresses. The 1920s became known as the Roaring Twenties.

People listened to the new sounds of jazz. Musicians, artists, and writers tried out wonderful new styles.

Many families bought their first car during the 1920s. Cars gave people freedom to go wherever they wanted. By the late 1930s, Connecticut had its first highway—the Merritt Parkway.

Connecticut companies joined the rush to make new products. Pratt & Whitney began making airplane engines. Sikorosky Aircraft made helicopters. Bridgeport's factories made automobile parts and electrical appliances.

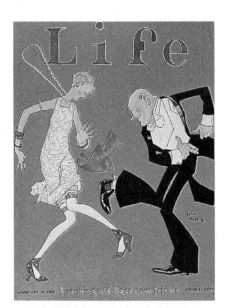

Connecticut's first radio station was WDRC. Families gathered around the radio to hear live programs.

New fashions and dances were part of the Roaring Twenties. Women who wore the new shorter dresses and had their hair "bobbed" (cut short) were called "flappers."

These men played on the Hartford Fire Department's softball team.

The Harlem Renaissance

African American painters, writers, and dancers celebrated black culture. They wanted to show that black was beautiful. Their work focused on life in Harlem, a black community in New York City. This was called the Harlem Renaissance. A *renaissance* is a re-birth, or new beginning.

Problems in the 1920s

Prohibition

The 1920s were a time of fun and excitement, but there were growing problems. One problem was alcohol. Some people thought drinking alcohol was a bad thing. They thought all whiskey, beer, and wine should be illegal. They wanted laws that said no one could make, sell, or drink alcohol.

The United States did make alcohol illegal for a while. People called it Prohibition because the government *prohibited* people from making and selling alcohol.

During Prohibition, policemen who found liquor often dumped it down the sewer.

Women Win the Right to Vote!

Women had been struggling to win the right to vote. Finally, in 1920, the Nineteenth Amendment was added to the Constitution. It gave women across America the right to vote.

Soon after, Connecticut women organized the League of Women Voters. They wanted to elect female leaders and lawmakers. Women finally had a voice in our government.

Some people were happy about Prohibition. Others were angry. They wanted to drink whiskey, beer, and wine like they always had.

Criminals knew that people still wanted to drink alcohol. They made it secretly. They had nicknames for the illegal drink. They called it "hootch" and "bathtub gin." Gangsters fought each other for control of the alcohol trade.

Prohibition did not last. After fourteen years, alcohol was made legal again.

Prejudice

Another terrible problem during the 1920s was prejudice. *Prejudice* is judging people just by their race, religion, whether they are male or female, or whether they are rich or poor.

Many immigrants had come to Connecticut during World War I to work in the factories. Soldiers returning from the war saw that people from Europe and African Americans from the South had already taken all the jobs. Some people were very angry.

Some African Americans worked as porters or waiters on the railroad lines. They helped passengers load their bags or served them tea and coffee.

The Connecticut Adventu

Black soldiers came back from the war to find that they could not enjoy the freedom they had fought for. They still were not welcome in stores, hotels, or on public beaches.

Klan members wore white hoods to hide their faces. They did not want people to know who they were. They burned crosses to scare people.

The Ku Klux Klan

A group called the Ku Klux Klan blamed African Americans, Catholics, Jews, and immigrants for America's problems. They attacked immigrant workers. Angry mobs surrounded the homes of innocent African American families. They set fire to the homes. Sometimes they took the father away and beat him or killed him.

Most people in Connecticut and across the country thought the Klan was very un-American. They did not like the bad things it did. Groups such as the National Association for the Advancement of Colored People (NAACP) and the Urban League helped black people during these difficult times. So did churches, schools, and clubs.

Good Times and Bad Times

The Great Depression

Besides alcohol and prejudice, there were growing problems in business. Connecticut and the nation were moving toward some very hard times.

A *depression* is a time when many people can't make enough money to take care of their families. They want to work, but they can't find jobs. The depression of the 1930s was the worst depression the United States has ever known. That is why it is called the Great Depression.

The Stock Market Crash of 1929

People knew that businesses were in trouble on one terrible day. It happened in New York City at a place called Wall Street. People traded *stock* there. If you own stock, then you own part of a company. When business is good, stock prices go up. When business is bad, stock prices go down.

On October 29, 1929, people agreed that business was bad. They all started selling their stock. Stock prices fell. By the end of the day, most stocks were worthless. People said the stock market had "crashed."

Many banks had invested their money in stocks. When the stocks became worthless, the banks lost all their money. When people went to their banks to get their money, it wasn't there. Many people lost every penny they had saved.

People couldn't afford to buy radios and cars. They stopped buying new homes. This meant that factories did not need to make as much, so they sent workers home. Without paychecks, workers could no longer buy things. More businesses slowed down.

One out of every four workers in the United States had no job.

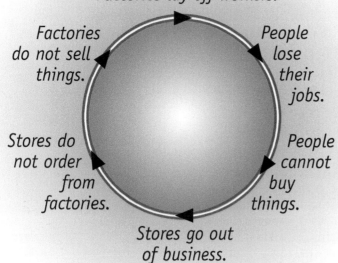

Depression Cycle

Factories lay off workers.

People lose their jobs.

People cannot buy things.

Stores go out of business.

Stores do not order from factories.

Factories do not sell things.

What do you think?

Stand up with all of your classmates and count off from one to four. Then have all the number ones sit down. That's the number of people who could not get a job during the Great Depression.

Discuss what it might feel like to have no way to earn money to pay for a home, food, or other things you need.

Minorities during the Depression

During this troubled time, some companies fired African Americans before they fired white workers. Women were often fired before men were. This was not fair, but this was what happened. It was one form of *discrimination*. The NAACP led men and women in protests to make things more equal.

How People Survived

Men sold apples on street corners to earn money. People stood in long lines to get free soup and bread. They grew gardens in their backyards. They mended old clothes.

These men were looking for work during the depression. Can you read their qualifications on their signs?

People waited in bread lines to get free food.
(Photo by Dorothea Lange)

"We ate potatoes three times a day—fried for breakfast, mashed at noon, and in potato salad for dinner. My mother even learned how to make potato fudge."

—*A child during the depression*

Many families lost their homes. Some people lived under bridges or made shelters out of scrap wood or metal. Many moved in with relatives.

People tried to help each other as much as they could. Sou kitchens served free meals to hungry people. Local police and firemen collected food and gave it to families who had no money. The Salvation Army, Red Cross, and many churches an synagogues all pitched in, but it was hard in Connecticut, just like everywhere else.

The New Deal

People began to wonder if the depression would ever end. They were worried that life would just get worse and worse. Then the government decided that it must take action.

President Franklin Roosevelt had a plan. He called his plar the New Deal. He started projects in order to create jobs. The government hired people to do all sorts of work.

"I pledge you, I pledge myself, to a new deal for the American people."
—*Franklin Delano Roosevelt*

President Roosevelt gave a radio speech every week. The talks were called "fireside chats." He sat near a fireplace in the White House with Falla, his little dog. It was as if the whole nation was sitting around the fire with him. He told Americans they could beat the depression if they worked together.

Alphabet Soup

Thousands of people went to work for the government. The new government programs were known by their initials. People called them "alphabet soup."

• **CCC: Civilian Conservation Corps.** The CCC put young men to work building and repairing parks across the country. They planted trees. They built public golf courses, playgrounds, and hiking trails. There were fourteen CCC camps in Connecticut.

CCC workers stand in line for dinner.

• **WPA: Works Progress Administration.** The WPA put men and a few women to work building new schools, post offices, roads, and bridges. It made state hospitals and prisons more modern. It built housing for students at state colleges. Artists painted murals on the walls of city buildings. The WPA paid actors to put on shows. It hired history experts to write local histories.

In Connecticut, WPA workers made state hospitals and prisons more modern. They made repairs at the State Capitol. They built a fish pond in New Fairfield.

• **NYA: National Youth Administration.** The NYA helped put 5,000 students to work. In Bridgeport, students were paid for putting books back on the shelves at the Bridgeport Public Library.

Connecticut Portrait

Marian Anderson
1897–1993

As a young girl, Marian Anderson loved to sing in the church choir. She grew up to become a wonderful opera singer.

Because Marian was African American, some concert halls did not let her sing there. In the late 1930s, even Constitution Hall in our nation's capital did not let her in. The first lady, Eleanor Roosevelt, did not like this. She invited Marian to sing at the Lincoln Memorial on Easter Sunday. Marian sang to an audience of 75,000 people.

Years later, in 1955, Marian Anderson made history. She became the first African American singer to perform with the Metropolitan Opera in New York City. She opened the way for many other black artists.

Marian Anderson lived the last half of her life in Danbury.

Nature Makes Matters Worse

The depression was not Connecticut's only problem during the 1930s. There were two natural disasters that made matters worse:

• The Connecticut River flooded its banks and put most of Hartford under water. Over 5,000 people lost their homes. A few people lost their lives.

• A hurricane hit just two years after the flood. Ocean waves were seventeen feet above normal. Large homes on the shore were destroyed. Tobacco growers and other farmers lost their crops. In Branford, a woman reading in her car was killed when a tree fell on the car. Eighty-five people in Connecticut lost their lives.

During the hurricane, a train got stuck in Stonington. To pass the time, the passengers crowded into two cars and had a party.

Windsor Street in Hartford was flooded after the hurricane.

A Second World War

While Americans were suffering through the depression, so were people in many other countries. President Roosevelt and the New Deal helped Americans get through those difficult years. Not all countries were as lucky.

In some places, dictators took over the government. A *dictator* is a ruler who has all of the power. Adolf Hitler was the dictator of Germany. Italy and Japan also had dictators.

The Connecticut Adventure

The dictators stopped holding elections. They had people who worked against the dictators killed or put in prison. In Japan, the dictator's army took over the government.

The rulers of those countries wanted to conquer their neighbors. When the German army invaded Poland, all of Europe went to war. On the other side of the world, Japan invaded China. Millions of people were murdered.

Attack at Pearl Harbor!

The United States did not get involved in the war for the first two years. Then something terrible happened in Hawaii.

The U.S. Navy had a base in Pearl Harbor, Hawaii. Many of our ships were there. One day in December, Japanese airplanes dropped bombs on the navy base. The bombs destroyed ships and killed people. The next day, the United States declared war on Japan.

Once again we were at war. We were fighting Germany, Italy, and Japan. On our side were England, France, and Russia.

People bought war bonds to raise money for the war. A bond was like a loan to the government. A family who bought it got more money back after the war was over.

Connecticut Portrait

Katharine Hepburn
1907–2003

People liked to forget their troubles by going to the movies. For a few hours, they could escape into the story or just watch the beautiful faces on the screen. One face that became famous was Katharine Hepburn's.

Hepburn grew up in Hartford and West Hartford. Her mother was well known for her work with women's rights. Her father was a doctor. She had four brothers and sisters.

As a young girl, Katharine put on plays with children in her neighborhood. When she grew up, she wanted to be an actress. Her father did not want her to become an actress, but Katharine was very *independent*. She made her own decisions.

Hepburn's first movies came out in the 1930s, but she made movies into the 1980s. She won four Academy Awards for "best actress."

Women went to work to help the war effort.

Connecticut in World War II

Connecticut sent over 200,000 men and women to serve in the war. Soldiers and sailors fought in countries around the world. They fought on ships in both the Atlantic and Pacific Oceans. Doctors and nurses took care of the wounded. Many women worked in army offices.

Once again, war orders came into Connecticut's factories. United Aircraft, Electric Boat Shipyard, and Sikorsky Aircraft were the main factories producing planes and ships for the war.

When the men left for war, they left their jobs behind. Someone had to take their places, so women moved into new types of work. They worked in factories. They worked as telephone operators. They ran streetcars and railroads.

Thousands of new workers came to Connecticut. The men and women who worked in the factories were just as important as the soldiers fighting overseas.

Children also did their part. They collected pots, pans, and tin cans that could be turned into metal for making ships.

Children collected rubber tires and metal.
These items were used to make things for the war.

Many families grew "victory gardens" so they would not have to buy things at the store. Then farmers could supply more food for the men and women in the armed forces. People drove only when they had to so they could save gas and rubber tires.

Rationing

One way to be sure that the soldiers had everything they needed was to limit what people at home could buy. People could buy only a small amount of sugar, meat, butter, coffee, gas, and tires.

Each family was given *ration* stamps to buy these items every month. When the stamps ran out, the family had to wait until the next month to buy more items.

Guarding the Home Front

Because airplanes could fly across the ocean and new bombs could go long distances, states along the coast were afraid of an air attack. Some people worked as airplane spotters. Their job was to watch for enemy planes. Connecticut had "blackouts," where everyone turned off their lights or hung shades in their windows. If an enemy pilot flew over the town, he would think no one was there because he couldn't see any lights. Volunteers patrolled the streets to make sure everyone was following the blackout rules.

No enemy planes ever dropped bombs on the East Coast. Children at home in Connecticut were safe.

The Holocaust

One terrible thing that happened during World War II was the *Holocaust.* Adolf Hitler believed that Germans were better than other people. He believed the world would be better with only one kind of people. He especially hated Jews. First he took away their rights. Then he tried to kill the Jews in all the countries he *conquered.*

These men were prisoners at a concentration camp. Women and children were also sent to the camps.

"Next year would have been my last year at school, but I won't be able to graduate . . . the schools have closed. . . . The Nazis have forced more than 5,000 Jews in Minsk [Russia] . . . to live in one small area of town."

—*A young Jewish girl*

Hitler's troops rounded up all the Jewish people. They put them into railroad cars and sent them to *concentration camps.* At the camps, there was hardly anything to eat. The people were forced to do hard labor. People who were too old, too young, or too weak to work were killed right away. About six million Jews died in these camps. Six million other people were also murdered because of their race or religion.

Some Jewish families in Connecticut still had relatives in Europe. They wondered what had happened to their loved ones.

When the war ended, American and European soldiers went to free the people in the concentration camps. They were horrified at what they saw. The survivors looked like walking skeletons. Entire families had been wiped out. Survivors spent a lifetime looking for lost relatives and friends.

The Connecticut Adventure

World War II Ends

After years of fighting and millions of deaths, World War II finally ended. The United States and its *allies* had defeated Germany. When news of the victory reached the United States, the people in Connecticut and all over America celebrated VE Day. VE stood for "Victory in Europe." Church bells rang and people paraded joyously through the streets.

Three months later, Japan surrendered. Americans celebrated VJ Day. VJ Day stood for "Victory in Japan." Once again the people of Connecticut celebrated. They were glad to see peace return. Everyone looked forward to better days.

The Atomic Bomb

During the war, countries on both sides tried to build a super bomb. The United States and England finally did it. Their scientists built the world's first *atomic bomb*. It was more powerful than any other bomb in history.

To end the war with Japan, the United States dropped an atomic bomb on Hiroshima, Japan. It completely destroyed the city in one terrible explosion. But Japan did not surrender.

A few days later, another plane dropped an atomic bomb on another Japanese city. It was a terrible thing for the Japanese people, but it ended the war with Japan. Luckily, these terrible weapons have never again been used in wartime.

American planes bombed cities in Europe and Japan. How is this small plane different from today's jets?

This mushroom cloud rose to over 60,000 feet above Japan.

Using Movies to Think about History

During the Great Depression, people loved to go to the movies to forget their troubles for a while. Your public library or local video stores might have some early "talking pictures." Choose a movie from the 1930s and watch some of it in your classroom.

Can you tell what the people who first watched these same motion pictures enjoyed?

If people were to watch our most popular movies seventy years from now, what are some things they would learn about us?

Your Own Interview

Interview someone who lived during World War II. Choose a great-grandparent, family friend, or neighbor.

Before the interview, get together with your class and make a list of questions you would like to ask. What kinds of things do you want to know? Here are some suggestions.

- How old were you when the war started?
- What do you remember most about the war?
- How were things different after the war ended?
- How might life be different today if the United States had not fought in the war?

Chapter 10 Review

1. List three things people did for fun during the Roaring Twenties.
2. What organization blamed America's problems on African Americans, Jews, Catholics, and immigrants?
3. What was the Great Depression?
4. What was the name of President Roosevelt's plan to put people back to work? How did the different jobs help both workers and other people?
5. What two natural disasters happened in Connecticut during the 1930s?
6. Why did the United States enter World War II?
7. How did the men, women, and children of Connecticut help the country during World War II?
8. What was the Holocaust?
9. What was VE Day?
10. What was VJ Day?

Geography Tie-In

The New Deal work projects changed our natural environment. Workers cleared out brush and built roads. They planted trees. They made campgrounds.

Make a list of ways your city or neighborhood has been changed from its natural state.

- Were the changes good for people?
- Were they good for animals?

Talk with your class about how you can improve the place where you live.

Chapter 11

THE TIME
1945–2000

PEOPLE TO KNOW
Ann Petry
Martin Luther King Jr.
Ella Grasso
Maria C. Sanchez
Abraham Ribicoff
Ralph Nader

PLACES TO LOCATE
Stamford
Greenwich
Bridgeport
New Haven
Hartford
Old Saybrook
Windsor Locks
New Britain
Winsted
Riverside
Long Island Sound
New York City
Georgia
Puerto Rico
Vietnam
Mexico
Cuba
China
Japan
Korea
Bosnia
Kosovo, Yugoslavia

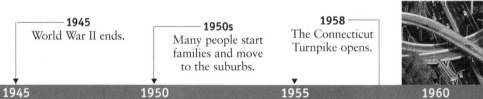

Timeline of Events

1945 World War II ends.

1950s Many people start families and move to the suburbs.

1958 The Connecticut Turnpike opens.

| 1945 | 1950 | 1955 | 1960 |

1950–1953 Korean War

1954 Connecticut launches the world's first nuclear-powered submarine.

Chapter 11

WORDS TO UNDERSTAND
aerospace
casino
civil rights
communism
commuter
consumer
defense
emissions
income tax
interstate
nuclear
pattern of settlement
preserve
suburb
vehicle

Modern Connecticut

1965
Connecticut adopts a new state constitution.

1963–1975
Vietnam War

1968
Martin Luther King Jr. is murdered in Tennessee.

1991
Connecticut gets a state income tax.

Persian Gulf War

2000
People across Connecticut celebrate a new millennium.

55   1970   1975   1990   1995   2000

1967–1969
Riots take place in the cities.

1974
Ella Grasso becomes the first female governor of Connecticut.

1960s
Civil Rights Movement

1990s
More and more people buy computers for their homes. E-mail and the Internet are widely used.

A Booming State and Nation

After World War II, thousands of men and women came home to Connecticut. They had served their country in many parts of the world. Now they could be with their families again.

To say "thank you" to soldiers who had served in the armed forces, the government paid for their education. This was called the G.I. Bill of Rights. Veterans could go to state colleges such as the University of Connecticut. They could learn to be carpenters or plumbers. They could also go to medical school. They could get loans so they could buy houses and start businesses.

Baby Boom

The world was at peace, and the future seemed safe. There seemed to be jobs for everyone. Families started having more babies. That's why adults who were born just after the war are called "baby boomers."

Larger families bought more goods. They needed more clothes, diapers, food, furniture, and houses. They also wanted larger and faster automobiles.

Families started buying televisions in the 1950s. All the shows were in black and white. Do your grandparents remember getting their first television?

Cars and Highways

Advertisements were changing people's minds about how many cars they needed. The ads said one car was enough for work, but a second car was needed to take children to school and pick up groceries.

With all the new cars came new roads and highways. The government built a new kind of highway that connected one state with another. It was called an *interstate*.

Linking the past to the present

Today, interstates are filled with cars, buses, and trucks. Look at a road map of Connecticut. Can you find I-91 and I-95? You can follow them from state to state.

Your grandparents might have driven a car like this in 1947.

People used cars like this to drive from their homes in the suburbs to their jobs in the cities in 1954.

(Photo by Middleton Evans)

The Suburbs

Cars and highways let people live farther away from where they worked. They could drive to work and then drive home after work. The areas outside the cities, with rows and rows of houses, are called *suburbs*.

Towns such as Stamford and Greenwich quickly became suburbs of New York City. Bridgeport, New Haven, Hartford, and most other large cities have suburbs today. Can you name some of them?

By 1960, Connecticut was one of the nation's richest states.

Economic Boom

Connecticut's economy grew after the war. The biggest industry was the *defense* industry. The defense industry included companies that made weapons, *vehicles*, and other items for war.

Why did we need a defense industry if the war was over? The reason was that the United States and Russia were enemies. They did not go to war, but both sides wanted to be prepared just in case. This was called the Cold War.

Sikorsky Aircraft Company got orders from the government to build military helicopters. Connecticut started to produce machines that used nuclear power. *Nuclear* power comes from atoms, or tiny chemical particles. United Aircraft Corporation led the state in *aerospace* products, missiles, and nuclear machines. It employed more people than any other company in Connecticut.

Sikorsky Aircraft Company built helicopters for the armed forces.

Changing Patterns of Settlement

Think back to what you learned about geography. What kinds of things affect where people settle? Natural features such as rivers and elevation affect where people live. People also like to live near good schools, stores, and businesses where they can get jobs.

The *patterns of settlement* changed in Connecticut during this time. It became cheaper to live in older apartments in the cities. Many poor families moved into the cities. Many middle-class and wealthy families left the cities to live in the suburbs.

When so many families moved out of the cities and into the suburbs, city life changed. Fewer people went downtown to shop. Since fewer people bought things in the city, business slowed down. Department stores, movie theaters, hotels, and restaurants moved into shopping malls in the suburbs.

The suburbs were growing. Companies such as Xerox, Champion International, and Olin-Matheson moved to suburban towns. They set up their headquarters in Stamford, Greenwich, and other places.

Many Puerto Rican families settled in the cities.
(Photo by Geoffrey Bluh)

Cleaning up the Cities

Most of Connecticut's cities wanted to fix up their downtown areas. During the 1950s and 60s, they started new projects. In New Haven, workers tore down slums and built new apartment buildings. A new road, the Oak Street Connector, linked downtown to I-95 and I-91. This made it easier for people to come into the city to work and shop. The Chapel Square Mall opened in the city. In Hartford, Constitution Plaza was built in an old part of town.

The new buildings brought some people back to the cities to work, but people still lived and shopped in the suburbs. For a while, the cities were still home to the poorest families.

Ann Petry
1908–1997

Ann Petry was born in Old Saybrook. She grew up in a neighborhood where many white people lived. Her father owned his own drugstore. Her mother was a foot doctor. Ann loved to listen to her mother's stories of how her ancestors struggled against racism.

Ann Petry started writing plays and stories in high school. Later, she wrote a book called *The Street*. In it, she wrote about the problems black women faced in the cities. She was one of the first black women to write about these things. *The Street* became very popular.

The women work because for years now the white folks haven't liked to give black men jobs that paid enough for them to support their families. . . . The men get out of the habit of working and the houses are old and gloomy and the walls press in.
—from *The Street*

The Civil Rights Movement

For many years, blacks and whites in much of America were separated, or segregated. In the South, there were separate schools for black children and white children. Black people had to sit in the back of buses and trains. They were allowed into some movie theaters, but they had to sit in the balcony. Signs saying "white only" or "colored only" hung above water fountains and lunch counters.

In Connecticut, African Americans were not welcome in certain neighborhoods. Many lived in the poorest parts of the cities. Banks would not give loans to black people.

Young African American leaders worked hard to end segregation. One leader was Dr. Martin Luther King Jr., a Baptist minister from Georgia. He organized peaceful protests and led marches against segregation. He reminded everyone that our nation was founded on the belief that "all men are created equal."

People invited Dr. King to speak in city after city. Many black people and some white people joined his marches and worked for civil rights. *Civil rights* are the basic rights that every citizen of our country is supposed to have.

Dr. Martin Luther King Jr. had a dream. He dreamed of freedom for all people of color.

Civil Rights in Connecticut

Many people did not understand just how badly blacks were being treated. Then television news shows started showing policemen attacking the protesters. People did not like what they saw. They saw that prejudice was still a huge problem.

Some people from Connecticut went to southern states to march and join the protests. They invited Martin Luther King Jr. and other leaders to visit Connecticut.

People knew they needed to change things in our state. The difference between life in the cities and life in the suburbs was too great. There was a lot of prejudice from both blacks and whites.

Later, a very sad thing happened. Dr. King was murdered in Memphis, Tennessee. Americans were shocked and sad. Black people were angry that he was killed just because he was trying to solve the problems of discrimination and poverty.

Riots broke out in several cities. Black teenagers told police, "You killed Martin Luther King!" Even in New Haven, where people had worked to fix problems in the city, windows were broken and fires were set. The mayor of New Haven said, "If we are a model city, God save the rest of the cities."

This man is lying down as a peaceful way of protesting. The police are moving him away from the door.

The Civil Rights Act of 1964

Finally, the courts stepped in and made it clear that all people should be treated equally. As Martin Luther King had said, only a person's character—not his or her color—should count.

Project Concern

People worked to bring blacks and whites together quickly. They tried a new plan in the schools. Some black students were bused to the suburbs to go to school with white children. Some white students were bused to black schools in the cities. This was called Project Concern.

Some people were against Project Concern. Busing students to a school far away from home caused problems. But many people believed it helped to bring the two groups together.

Churches taught people how to treat each other. Colleges tried to include black students and teachers. They offered classes in black history, race relations, and city problems.

Maria C. Sanchez
1926–1989

Maria Sanchez was born in Puerto Rico. She came to Hartford in 1953.

Maria wanted to help the Hispanic people of Hartford. She started "Maria's News Stand" on a corner in the city. From her newsstand she helped people find homes, jobs, and good schools.

Maria Sanchez started the Puerto Rican Parade Committee. She worked for La Casa de Puerto Rico and other groups that helped Hispanics.

Maria was the first Hispanic woman elected to the General Assembly. There she helped make laws for Connecticut.

Maria Sanchez is known as the "godmother" of the Hispanic Community. She even has an elementary school in Hartford named for her. It is the Maria C. Sanchez Elementary School.

The Women's Movement

At the same time that blacks were fighting for their civil rights, women of all races were fighting for equal rights with men. Many women in Connecticut and the rest of the nation joined together to start the Women's Movement. They worked to win equal pay for equal work. They wanted women to have the same opportunities in jobs and education that men had.

Connecticut was the first state in the nation to elect a female governor. A governor is the leader of a state. Ella Grasso was chosen to lead Connecticut.

Some women in Connecticut did not like the Women's Movement. They said that women already had the same rights as men had. Other people said that a woman's main job was to be a wife and mother. If all the women in Connecticut went to work, they asked, what would become of the children? Other people worried that if everything was equal, women would have to fight in wars, right along with the men.

Many women wanted to pass an amendment to the Constitution called the Equal Rights Amendment, or ERA. The women in this photo did not want the ERA. It did not pass in enough states to become part of the Constitution.

More Wars

Since the end of World War II, people from Connecticut have fought in the Korean War, the Vietnam War, the Persian Gulf War, in Afghanistan, and Iraq.

The Vietnam War was the longest war our country ever fought. It lasted over ten years. American troops went overseas to fight in Vietnam. They tried to keep the communists from taking over the government in South Vietnam. *Communism* is a form of government in which people cannot own property or choose where they will travel or where they will live. They do not get to vote for their leaders. They can't choose a religion. They don't have the freedom that we have.

Many Americans marched to protest the war. They believed our country was not fighting for a good reason. Other people thought it was important to stop communism from spreading.

Connecticut Portrait

Ella Grasso
1919–1981

Ella Grasso was born in Windsor Locks. Her parents were immigrants from Italy. She became Connecticut's first female governor and its first Italian governor.

Before she became governor, Ella Grasso served in the General Assembly. She also had served as Connecticut's secretary of state.

Governor Grasso was very popular. After saying the state should cut costs, she turned her words into action. She returned a raise of $7,000 she had gotten from the state. She also never forgot her immigrant roots and the needs of working families.

During the blizzard of 1978, she worked all day and night to make sure the snowplows got out and made the streets safe.

When Ella Grasso died in 1981, bumper stickers saying "Thank You Ella" appeared on cars all over the state.

Are these protesters for or against the Vietnam War?

Connecticut Portrait

Abraham Ribicoff
1910–1998

Abraham Ribicoff was born in a tenement in New Britain. His parents were Jewish immigrants. He did not let being poor stop him from going after his dreams. He grew up to lead the state of Connecticut as its first Jewish governor.

Ribicoff became a lawyer, then a judge. He served in the General Assembly, then as a U.S. congressman.

Ribicoff spoke out against the Vietnam War. He wanted to fix the problems in the cities. After serving as governor, he became a United States senator.

Captain Lynn Been was surrounded by students after returning from Vietnam. He told them,

"The plane I was flying was shot down over a rice field. I landed safely with my parachute. Covered in mud from head to foot, I was tied up and led to a truck. Then I was taken to a prison. I was treated better than many other soldiers. They deserve glory, not me."

Taking Care of Our Environment

Many people are concerned that we are not taking good care of the world we live in. They are worried about how pollution hurts people and animals. They talk to our lawmakers and ask them to pass laws that are good for the environment.

Connecticut has passed some laws to help clean up the air we breathe. For example, all cars must pass an *emissions* test. A machine tests cars to make sure they do not pollute the air too much. Other laws tell industries what kinds of emissions they can and cannot put into the air.

Preserving the Sound

The people of Connecticut are working hard to restore the state to its natural beauty. One group is working to *preserve* Long Island Sound. They call their organization Save the Sound.

Save the Sound wants to preserve natural habitats for plants and animals. They want to put back, or restore, habitats that have been destroyed. Here are some things they want to do:
- Remove plants that are not native to the Sound.
- Plant more beach grasses on the dunes.
- Remove dams and other things that block the routes of fish in the rivers.

Sea Oats

Public Transportation

Cars pollute the air. They cause traffic jams. They are expensive to run. But many people who do not have cars find it hard to get around. The answer to these problems is good public transportation. Trains, buses, subways, and light rail systems are examples of public transportation.

Connecticut has *commuter* trains to move lots of people from place to place, in and out of the cities. You can take an express bus or ride in a carpool. When more people use trains and buses, there are fewer traffic jams. There is less air pollution. More public transportation will make our cities nicer places to live.

Commuters can catch a train at Old Greenwich Railroad Station.
(Photo by Scott Barrow)

Connecticut Portrait

Ralph Nader
1934–

What if you bought a car, but it wasn't made to be safe? What if the food you ate had gross things in it that you didn't know about? These are the kinds of things Ralph Nader wants to stop.

Nader became a lawyer and worked to protect consumers. A *consumer* is anyone who buys things.

Nader was born in Winsted. He first became famous in the 1960s when he wrote a book called *Unsafe at Any Speed*. The book helped get laws passed for seat belts and air bags in cars. He went on to help improve things like food products and health care.

Nader tries to stop pollution and get people to take care of the environment. You may recognize his face—he ran for president of the United States in 2004.

An End to the Boom

At the end of the 1980s, the country started cutting back on defense. There was not as much work to be done in the defense industry. Colt Firearms Company went out of business. Companies like United Technologies and the Electric Boat Shipyard laid off thousands of workers. The cuts hurt the economy of Connecticut.

Connecticut's population began to shrink. Young people left the state to find jobs in other places. Retired people moved to warmer states where taxes and prices were lower.

To help raise money, the state started an income tax in 1991. An *income tax* is a tax on the money every person earns. Even with the new tax, it took the economy almost ten years to recover. By 2000, it was doing well again.

Recent Immigrants

Today, people continue to come to Connecticut to live. They come from all over the world. They work to make a good life in their new home.

Hispanics

Thousands of Puerto Rican immigrants have moved to Connecticut over the last fifty years. Many came to work on tobacco farms. When the tobacco industry slowed down, they had to find new jobs. Many moved to cities such as Bridgeport, New Haven, and Hartford.

Hispanic people have come from other countries, too. They have left their homes in Mexico, Cuba, and countries in South America to make new lives in our state.

Asians

More and more Asian families are settling in Connecticut. They come from countries such as China, Japan, Korea, Thailand, and Vietnam.

Like many ethnic groups, Asians have faced discrimination. They often had to take the jobs no one else wanted. They have worked hard to make a good life for themselves in Connecticut.

Native Americans Return

An important group is returning to Connecticut after a long absence. Many Native Americans are living in Connecticut once again. After their ancestors were forced to leave Connecticut long ago, the people have come back to the land they once called home.

The Mashantucket Pequots opened a *casino* resort called Foxwoods on their reservation in 1992. Foxwoods became a popular place to visit. With the money they earned, the Pequots have improved their reservation and built a museum. Mohegan Indians also run a successful casino near Uncasville.

Eastern Europeans

Many immigrants have come from places like Bosnia and Yugoslavia because war has destroyed their towns. They are building a new life here in their new country.

Some of Connecticut's immigrants come from countries in Asia. This mother and baby are from a country called Laos.

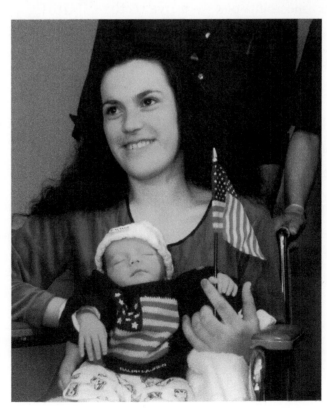

This mother named her baby Amerikan. He was born just after his parents came from Kosovo, Yugoslavia, to escape war.

Citizenship: Don't Take It for Granted!

Many immigrants study to become citizens of the United States. They work all day and then to go classes in the evening to learn English. They also learn the American way of life.

When they are ready, immigrants take a test. They answer questions about American history and government. If they pass, they promise to live according to the laws of America and their state. There is usually a ceremony in the county courthouse. It is a very proud moment for the new Americans.

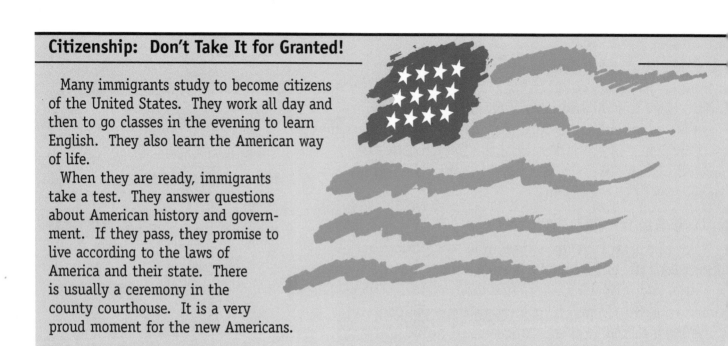

Chapter 11 Review

1. How did automobiles help people move to the suburbs?
2. What was the biggest industry in Connecticut in the 1950s?
3. What have some Connecticut cities done to make the downtown areas nicer?
4. What are civil rights?
5. Give two examples of groups fighting for civil rights during this time period.
6. How did Ella Grasso serve Connecticut?
7. What was the longest war in American history? How long did it last?
8. What are some ways people are preserving Long Island Sound?
9. Name three kinds of public transportation. How do they help our environment?
10. Name three countries from which immigrants have come in the past fifty years.

Activity

Local Communities

1. Locate your community on a map of Connecticut.

   - What kind of community do you live in?
   - Who are some of the people who live there?
   - Where are they from?
   - What kinds of things do people do to make a living?
   - Where do they go to have fun?
   - What kinds of ethnic foods do they eat?
   - What kinds of businesses are in your town or city?

2. On the map, locate some of the communities that surround yours. Describe what they are like. How are they different from your community?

3. Divide your class into groups. With your group, choose a nearby community and prepare a report on it. Share your report with your class. Put the class reports together to make a book of the places around you.

Geography Tie-In

The United States went to war several times after World War II. Our soldiers fought in Korea, Vietnam, and the Persian Gulf. Locate these places on a world map. On what continents are they located?

Chapter 12

Chapter

Our State Government

12

WORDS TO UNDERSTAND
ambassador
candidate
district
jury
local government
nominate
ordinance
selectmen
veto

Our freedom is protected by both our national and our state governments.
(Photo by Scott Barrow)

Government for Connecticut

The fifty states of our country have different geography, people, and industries. Each state has different problems. Each state has its own state government to solve these problems. For example, in the West, Arizona and Utah make laws about how water can be used. Water is very important there because they are desert states. West Virginia makes laws about safety in its coal mines.

Connecticut's government makes laws about fishing in our rivers and lakes and on Long Island Sound. It tries to prevent pollution from entering the waterways and the air.

Like the national government, the state government is divided into three branches. Each branch has certain duties. This way the power is balanced. Balancing power is a very important part of our government.

Legislative Branch

In Connecticut, the legislative branch is called the General Assembly. It is made up of the state Senate and the House of Representatives. They make the laws for Connecticut.

Connecticut lawmakers meet at the State Capitol Building in Hartford.

People from all over Connecticut vote for their favorite representatives. Then the people tell their representatives how they feel about issues. They write them letters, call them on the phone, send them e-mail, or talk to them in person.

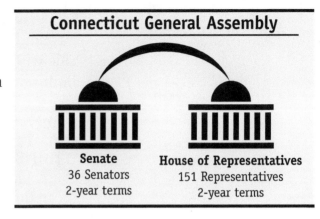

Connecticut General Assembly

Senate
36 Senators
2-year terms

House of Representatives
151 Representatives
2-year terms

Executive Branch

The governor is the head of the state executive branch. The governor is elected by the people of Connecticut. Here is a list of some jobs the governor does:

- Sees that state laws are carried out.
- Suggests new laws to the General Assembly.
- Prepares a state budget.
- Signs new laws or *vetoes* them.
- Calls the General Assembly into special extra meetings.
- Appoints people to run state programs.
- Acts as the commander in chief of the state units of the National Guard.
- Grants pardons (forgiveness) to people found guilty of crimes.

Many people help the governor in the executive branch. Some collect tax money. Others help people get licenses to drive cars or run businesses. Workers in the executive branch help farmers market their products. They inspect farm animals to be sure they are healthy. Others work for our state parks and roads, or in health or education.

Judicial Branch

The courts make up the third branch of our state government. Courts decide who is right when people disagree about what a law means. Courts also decide if a person is guilty of a crime.

The judge and often a *jury* listen to reports of police officers. They listen to other people who might have been involved. After everyone has been heard, the jury must decide if the person on trial is guilty or innocent. If the person is found guilty of the crime, the judge decides how the person should be punished.

In another kind of case, a person might feel that he or she has not been treated fairly. A person might ask the court to decide who was to blame for an accident. The court will listen to both sides and then decide on a way to settle the argument.

Activity

You Be the Judge!

A judge is a very important person. He or she must listen carefully to both sides before deciding what to do. The judge can fine people, send people to jail, or just talk to them about being good citizens. In each case, a judge uses the laws that were written by the legislators to decide what to do.

Now it is your turn to be a judge. Read the story below. Then write how you would have these boys settle their problem.

Jason loves to practice tricks on his new skateboard after school. When he is finished, he always takes it inside where it will be safe. One day his friend Matthew asks to borrow the board for a while. Jason agrees and tells Matthew to take good care of it and to bring it back before dark.

Matthew enjoys riding the skateboard and stays out late. When he goes home, it is getting dark and his family is calling him in for the night. Matthew lays the board down on the ground and goes in. In the morning, the skateboard is gone. It has been stolen.

Jason is very upset! He thinks Matthew's family should buy him a new one. Matthew says his family does not have enough money to buy one. He has never even had one himself. He says it was too dark to return the board the night before.

Matthew says he had planned to go back outside later and put it in a safe place, but he forgot. He says it was not his fault the skateboard was stolen.

The Connecticut Adventure

What Are Political Parties?

Political parties are groups of people who have a lot of the same ideas about government. Most people choose the Democratic Party or the Republican Party. Those are the two main parties in Connecticut and in the rest of the United States.

Some citizens do not belong to any party. They run for office or vote as Independents. They hardly ever win elections, but they do get a chance to say what they think is important.

To run for some government offices, a person must first be *nominated*, or named by a political party. A person who runs for office is called a *candidate.* Candidates raise money to make posters and buy TV and radio advertisements. They give speeches. At voting time, the people vote for the candidates they think will do the best job.

During elections, watch for these two animals on signs and badges: The elephant is the symbol for the Republicans. The donkey is the symbol for the Democrats.

Connecticut's Representatives

Representatives from around Connecticut meet to make state laws. Connecticut also sends representatives to Washington, D.C. to make laws for the whole country.

Two people from each state are elected to serve in the U. S. Senate. The federal government assigns the number of representatives for the state. Then our state government divides the cities into *districts* according to the number of representatives.

Who Can Vote?

Who can vote for representatives? Who can vote for the president of the United States and the governor of Connecticut?

Anyone can vote who is a citizen of the United States, is at least eighteen years old, and is registered (signed up) to vote.

Connecticut Portrait

Clare Boothe Luce
1903–1987

Back in the 1940s, Clare Boothe Luce was the first woman to represent Connecticut in the U.S. House of Representatives.

Before she moved to Connecticut, she lived in New York. She wrote plays and books. She worked for several fashion magazines. She also worked as a reporter during World War II.

After two terms as our congresswoman, Luce was chosen to represent our country in Italy. She was the first American woman to be an *ambassador* to a major country.

An ambassador is sent to another country to help both countries work peacefully together.

Representing the People

Joseph Lieberman represents Connecticut in the U.S. Senate. Before he became a U.S. senator, he served as a state senator. He is from Stamford.

In the year 2000, Lieberman ran for one of the highest jobs in the land—vice president of the United States. He did not win, but he was the first Jewish person to run for that important office.

Joseph Lieberman

Congresswoman Rosa DeLauro spends time reading with schoolchildren.

Rosa DeLauro works in the U.S. House of Representatives. She represents New Haven and the surrounding towns along the shoreline. She was raised in New Haven's Little Italy. Her grandmother owned a pastry shop there.

DeLauro started the Kick Butts Connecticut (KBC) program. It gets middle-school students to teach younger kids not to smoke. More than 2,000 children have taken the pledge not to smoke. She has involved high school students in the war on crime and violence through her Anti-Crime Youth Council.

Local Government

In some places in Connecticut, cows and horses roam the hills. In other places, skyscrapers and apartment buildings are all you see. Because different places in our state have different needs, *local governments* are important. Local governments are governments close to home.

Town and City Governments

Cities are usually run by a mayor or a city manager with a city council. Cities make rules about what kinds of buildings can be built in different regions of the city. They often keep houses separate from businesses. They make sure schools are in safe places. They make laws about speed limits on the roads. Cities also have city courts.

Most small towns are led by *selectmen*. The town's voters choose the selectmen to lead their town meetings.

Capital Cities

- The capital of the United States is Washington, D.C.
- The capital of Connecticut is Hartford.

Government representatives meet and make laws for our state and country in the capital cities.

People who live in Connecticut have to follow the rules of both the government of the United States and the government of Connecticut.

Levels of Government

In addition to branches of government, there are levels of government. Study the chart to see how this works.

- What level of government includes the mayor of your town or city?
- What level of government includes our governor?
- At what level of government does the president of the United States work?

Level	Place	Head of Executive Branch
Local	City, Town	Mayor
State	Connecticut	Governor
National	United States	President

What do you think?

Can you think of town or city laws that affect you? The laws are sometimes called *ordinances.* They might have to do with speed limits, crosswalks, dog licenses, garbage pick-up, buses or taxis, or rules for your park or swimming pool.
- Why do you think these ordinances were passed?
- Which ordinances do you agree with?
- Which ones would you like to change? Why?

Counties

For over 300 years, Connecticut had county governments. We no longer have county governments, but Connecticut is still divided into eight counties.

When you watch the weather report on the six o'clock news, you often hear about the different counties. Your county may still have a library or courthouse for the people in your community.

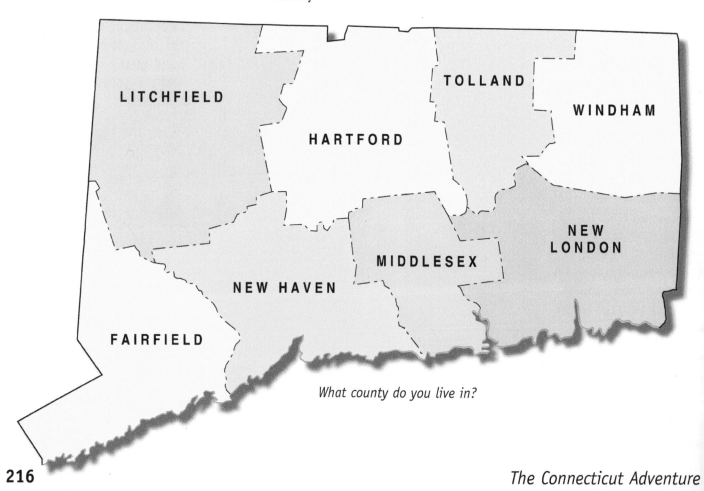

What county do you live in?

Taxes Pay for Services

Our state constitution gives the state, county, and city governments the power to collect taxes. Tax money pays for the services that governments provide.

Taxes come in many forms. People and businesses pay taxes on their income. When you buy new clothes or toys at stores, you pay a sales tax. Our license plate fees and turnpike tolls are also a kind of tax.

What is tax money used for? Taxes pay for fixing local streets and for plowing snow. Taxes pay for libraries where you can check out books. They pay for parks where you can play ball and have picnics. Towns and cities arrange for a clean water supply and have your garbage picked up. If you go to a public school, your school building, your books, and even your teacher are paid for with tax money.

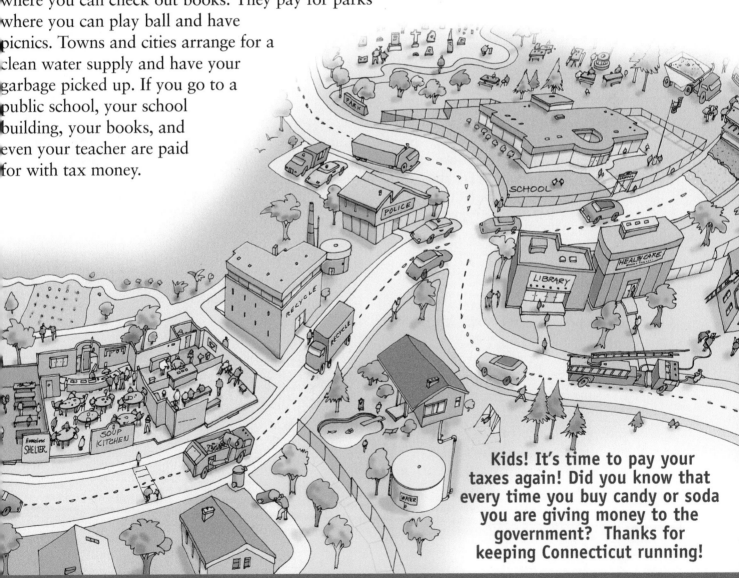

Kids! It's time to pay your taxes again! Did you know that every time you buy candy or soda you are giving money to the government? Thanks for keeping Connecticut running!

I'll Do It!

Volunteers are very important to a town or city. Volunteers work without being paid. They work in hospitals. They teach reading and English. They take care of children and take food to older people or people with disabilities. They give tours at museums. They play music in schools and give programs at homes for the elderly. Volunteers pick up trash and plant flowers and trees. Have you ever been a volunteer?

Each person should do his or her part to help other people and to solve problems. What are some of the problems in your community? As a class, choose one problem and think about how you or adults might help solve it. List your ideas on the chalkboard. Then do your part to make your community better.

Activity

Be a Good Citizen!

Connecticut is only as good as its people. That means all of the people—men and women, rich and poor, young and old—must be good citizens. They need to get involved in government and help others whenever they can.

Here are some things you can do. Discuss these ideas as a class. What other things can you do? Make a list on the board.

- Obey all of your family and school rules.
- Tell the truth.
- Be polite and helpful to everyone.
- Help keep your own home and yard clean.
- Never litter.
- Never ruin someone else's property.
- Ask adults in your family to vote.
- Tell your representatives what you want them to do (by letter or e-mail).
- Write a letter to the editor of a newspaper. Letters from kids often get published!
- Talk with adults about what is going on in government, especially in your town.

Chapter 12 Review

1. List the three branches of government.
2. A _____ or a _____ decides if a person is guilty of a crime.
3. We elect _____ to vote for us in government meetings.
4. Who are our United States senators from Connecticut?
5. A _____ is when the governor refuses to sign a bill.
6. Name the two main political parties.
7. Since Connecticut does not have county government, what kind of local government does it have?
8. What are some services that towns and cities provide?
9. List at least three things that tax money is used for.
10. Describe a good citizen.

VOTING BOOTH

Geography Tie-In

On a wall map in your classroom, locate Washington, D.C. (our national capital), and Hartford (our state capital).
- How far do our representatives have to travel to get to Washington?
- What are some of the ways they might travel? What states might they drive through or fly over?

Making a Living in Connecticut

Chapter 13

WORDS TO UNDERSTAND

capitalistic
consumer
economics
employee
entrepreneur
expense
free enterprise
good
livestock
non-profit
profit
salary
service
supply and demand
tourism
wage

The people of Connecticut are hard at work.
(Photo by Kindra Clineff)

Economics for Everyone

People have needs. They need food, water, clothing, and shelter. People also have wants. They want things like cars, books, toys, and bicycles. These are called *goods,* or products.

People also need medical care from doctors and nurses. They need education from teachers. They may want help repairing their washing machine or fixing a broken window. These are called *services.*

Economics is the study of how people get the goods and services that they need and want. An economic system is a way of producing and selling these goods and services.

Free Enterprise

There are many different economic systems. Different countries in the world use different systems. The United States has what is called a *capitalistic* or *free enterprise* system. Here is how it works:

• People own factories and companies that produce goods and services. In other systems, the government owns these things.

• Business owners get to decide what to produce and how much to charge for it. They decide where to do business. They decide who they want to help them. They are also in charge of selling the product.

• Business owners hire people called *employees* to work for them. The owner pays the employees a *wage* or a *salary.*

What do you think?

In some countries, the government owns all or part of the businesses. There is no free enterprise system. Talk with your teacher and other adults to compare our economic system with economic systems in other countries.

A good employee must be trained, come to work on time, work hard, get along with the other workers, and do the job he or she was hired to do.

Making a Profit

How do business owners make money? Usually they sell what the workers produce. They can sell goods or services. The grocery store sells food. Dentists sell their services to fix your teeth.

A *profit* is the money a business earns after it subtracts *expenses*. People who make cars have to pay for the steel, glass, and tires. These are expenses. They also have to pay their employees to make cars. So, they must sell the cars for more than it costs to make them. If not, they will have a loss instead of a profit. Soon they will be out of business.

People use money to buy the things they need and want. The work they do to earn money allows them to buy the things they need. Do you earn money? Do you spend it wisely?

Work and Play

What is work? Work is something we do to earn money or to get things done. Do you have to mow the lawn, take out the trash, clean your room, or walk the dog to earn your allowance? If you do, you are being paid for the work you do.

Do you rake the leaves or help dry the dishes? If so, you are working to make the yard or kitchen clean.

Homework is also a type of work. You do your homework so you can learn new things.

What is play? Play is all the fun things we do when we are not working. We ride our bikes, go swimming, swing on the swing set, watch movies, or play with toys. Of course, it is important to finish our work before we play. What do you like to play?

Supply and Demand

How do business owners decide how much to charge for their products? The selling price depends on a lot of things. The business has to make a profit. Sometimes the price depends on how much of something there is. If a toy becomes so popular that a company cannot make enough for everyone who wants it, the company can sell the toy for a higher price. People will be willing to pay more to get it. This is called the rule of *supply and demand.*

If a store has too many basketballs, the balls might go on sale.

Sometimes a company has to lower its prices. Maybe a company makes bicycles and tries to sell them at a certain price, but people don't buy very many of them. The company has a lot of extra bicycles sitting around. They might lower the price to get people to buy them.

Maybe there are two companies that make bicycles. One of the companies might lower its price to get people to buy from it instead of from the other company.

Sometimes there is only one company that produces a certain product. Then the owners can charge about whatever price they want. If buyers want that product or service, they will have to pay whatever price the company charges.

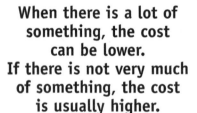

When there is a lot of something, the cost can be lower. If there is not very much of something, the cost is usually higher.

Consumers Buy Goods and Services

People are workers. They are also *consumers*. Anyone who spends money is a consumer. Are you a consumer? What kinds of things do you buy with your money?

People want to spend their money wisely. They compare different brands. They compare the prices at different stores. They also want to make sure that what they buy is really what they want.

Advertising

Businesses use advertising to get consumers to buy their products and services. Advertising may be on the radio, on TV, on the Internet, in newspapers and magazines, and even on billboards along highways. You see and hear it everywhere.

Does seeing this ad for Wild Things Sunglasses make you want to buy a pair?

Methods Used in Advertising

Here are some methods used in advertising to get you to buy:
1. **Color and excitement:** The ad is bright and colorful so people will notice it. The product seems fun and exciting.
2. **Repetition:** The ad says a name or slogan over and over.
3. **Social appeal:** The ad suggests that if you use a certain product you will be nice looking and have a lot of friends.
4. **Humor:** People like and remember things that are funny.
5. **Music:** People remember short tunes and jingles.

Activity

Write an Advertisement
Think of something you would like to advertise, then write a magazine or radio ad for it. Use some of the methods listed above in your ad.

A Wise Consumer

Advertising is important to business and important to the people who work for the company. Remember, a business has to make a profit. It has to sell what it produces. If the consumers don't know about a product, will they buy it?

Being a wise consumer means understanding how advertising works. Have you ever bought something because the advertisements made it seem exciting, but then you found out it wasn't? Do you always believe everything a commercial says?

Economics in Early Connecticut

Today, Connecticut has a free enterprise system like everywhere else in the United States. However, a system of free enterprise did not always exist here.

American Indians did not believe in private ownership of land. They believed the Great Spirit had made the land for everyone. No one had the right to own land and keep it. The land was to be shared by the people in the tribe.

When the Dutch came to Connecticut, they traded with the Indians. They gave the Indians guns, blankets, and pots and pans. In return, the Indians gave the Dutch furs and land. The Dutch sold the furs in Europe. They made a great profit. The Puritans who followed gave the Indians glass, brass, and cloth. In return, the Indians gave them furs and land.

The colonists who came to Connecticut wanted to buy land for farms. They grew corn, squash, and apples. They raised horses, cows, and pigs. They sold these goods and made a profit. Then they bought household items and farming equipment. Stores that sold these goods opened up in towns throughout the state. Soon Connecticut's economic system was much like that in other places in the country.

Immigrants Become Entrepreneurs

Some immigrants became entrepreneurs. An *entrepreneur* is someone who has an idea and the courage to start a business. Entrepreneurs work for themselves. Sometimes the whole family helps with the business. Even the children do small jobs for the family business.

Many immigrants began their businesses with a skill they had learned in their old country. Maybe an Irish woman who knew how to sew would fix coats and hem pants for her neighbors to earn extra money. If a group of furniture makers from Germany started a business, they could make more tables, chairs, and cupboards. Together they could have a good business.

Opening a restaurant was another way immigrants made money. Italian immigrants knew a lot about growing and preparing food. They opened delis and other food shops.

Some entrepreneurs sold services. They delivered groceries, painted homes, and taught classes. They opened their own barbershops and cut hair. Other immigrant entrepreneurs bought and sold goods. Some Jewish immigrants opened stores in cities around Connecticut.

Irish Workers

When Irish immigrants came to Connecticut, they got jobs working for other people. They built most of the roads, canals, and train tracks in the state. It was a hard way to live. But they were willing to take the jobs that no one else wanted to do.

The Irish sent their children to school. Their children studied hard and became teachers, doctors, lawyers, politicians, and clergymen. The Irish showed all the other immigrants who came after them how to survive in America.

Irish women did laundry to earn extra money.

Connecticut Entrepreneurs

Many people from Connecticut have started successful businesses. Let's meet two famous Connecticut entrepreneurs!

Paul Newman

Paul Newman is an actor who lives in Westport. One Christmas, he decided that if his salad dressing recipe was good enough for his friends, then it was good enough for the public. He started a company called Newman's Own and decided to give all of the profits to charity.

At first, Newman made only salad dressing. The experts told him he should expect to lose a million dollars in the first year. Instead, he made over a million dollars that first year.

If we'd followed the experts' advice, we'd probably still be bottling the dressing in our basement. . . . Instead, we followed our instincts and eighteen years later, company sales are stronger than ever.

Today, the company makes salad dressing, popcorn, pasta sauce, steak sauce, lemonade, and salsa. Paul Newman believes that he is successful because the products taste great and are all natural.

Fred Deluca

When Fred Deluca was a young man, he had to earn his own money. He said, "Back then . . . kids pretty much figured out how to make their own way." Fred made his own way by finding new customers on his paper route:

> *I passed by lots of doors that were not my customers.*
> *[I decided] I have to sell to these people because it doesn't take any more time to drop the papers in front of their doors—I'm walking by anyway.*

Fred Deluca was just seventeen when he started his first business. It was 1965, and he was looking for a way to make money to pay for college.

Fred discussed his desire to go to college with a family friend, Dr. Peter Buck. Dr. Buck suggested that opening a sandwich shop would help him earn enough money to pay for his education. He lent Fred the money, and they became partners. The first shop was called Pete's Super Submarines.

Today there are Subway restaurants all over the world. Everyone who sets up a Subway restaurant must follow the company's rules for making sandwiches. Fred Deluca learned what worked best and what did not work. He learned what people like.

Activity

Entrepreneurs in Your Community

Do you know any entrepreneurs in your community? Do you have a favorite store, business, or restaurant in your town? See if you can find out who started the business. Ask the entrepreneur what it took to get started.

Land (Natural Resources)

In economics, the term "land" means anything found in nature. If you are making chairs, you might use wood. If you are makin[g] teddy bears, you may need cotton to stuff them. Cotton an[d] wood are both natural resources that grow on the land[.] Machines need energy. This energy can come fro[m] coal, oil, the sun, and even the wind. They a[re] natural resources, too.

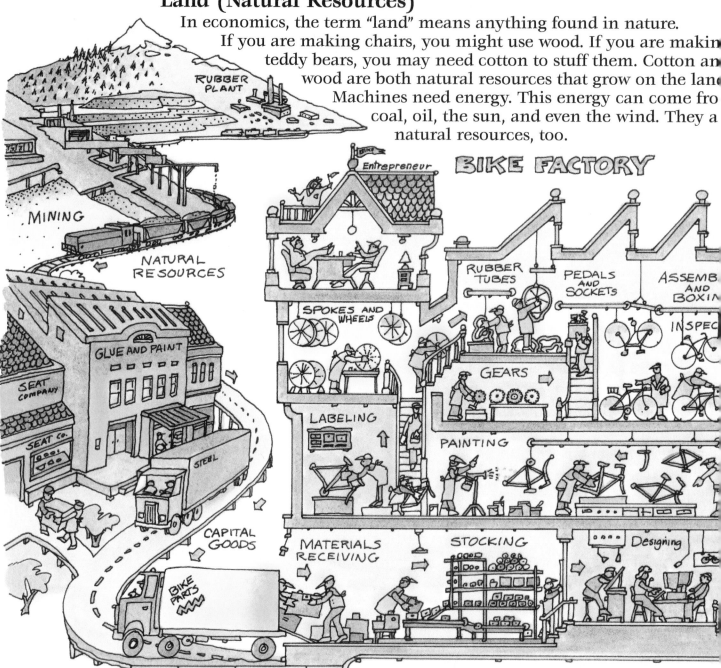

Capital Goods

When you use things that are already made to make something else, you are using capital goods. A carpenter doesn't make his own hammer—he just uses it to build a house. The hammer and nails a carpenter uses are capital goods. The money you need to start and run a business is also called capital.

Entrepreneurship

Entrepreneurship means owning and running a business. It often starts with an idea. The person must be willing to take a risk to make the idea work. Entrepreneurs use natural resources, capital goods, and labor to make mone[y.]

Factors of Production

There are four things that must come together before something is sold as a good or service. These things are called factors of production. Factors of production are land, capital goods, entrepreneurship, and labor.

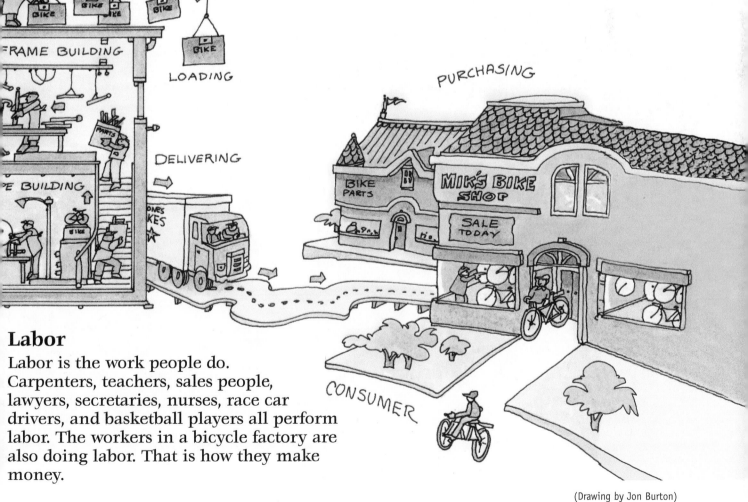

Labor

Labor is the work people do. Carpenters, teachers, sales people, lawyers, secretaries, nurses, race car drivers, and basketball players all perform labor. The workers in a bicycle factory are also doing labor. That is how they make money.

(Drawing by Jon Burton)

Transportation and Trade

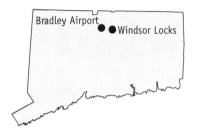

Transportation is very important for business. Natural resources and finished products are brought into Connecticut. In return, Connecticut ships products out to places around the world. We ship out machines, computer equipment, chemicals, rubber, paper, and many other products. Without good transportation, business would almost stop.

Airports: Connecticut's major airport is Bradley International Airport in Windsor Locks. It serves most of Connecticut and western New England. Bradley is the second busiest airport in New England. Smaller airports are in Bridgeport, New Haven, Oxford, and Groton.

Ships bring goods in and out of the port at Groton.
(Photo by Scott Barrow)

The Connecticut Adventure

Railroads: Trains still crisscross the state just like they did more than 100 years ago. Some trains bring goods into Connecticut and take manufactured items out of the state. The largest of these is the Consolidated Rail Corporation (Conrail).

Passenger trains carry thousands of workers into New York City each day. Amtrak carries passengers to towns along the shore and to Springfield and Boston, Massachusetts. The Shore-Line East carries people from New London to New Haven.

Roads and Highways: Roads have been important to Connecticut since the early days of settlement. The first roads were trails the Indians made through the woods. Over time, the trails became roads that wagons and carriages could use. Much later, the roads were paved for cars. Road-building never stopped in Connecticut. Today, major interstates and the Boston Post Road link Connecticut to the rest of the nation.

Waterways: Long Island Sound and the Connecticut River provided a way for the first settlers to come to Connecticut. These waterways are still important to the people of our state. Boats and small barges carry oil and gasoline to Hartford. Oils and chemicals are stored at New Haven. Our shoreline on Long Island Sound has many excellent harbors and ports such as Bridgeport, New London, Stamford, and Norwalk. Ferries take people from Bridgeport and New London to Long Island.

Activity

The World in Your Closet

You are an important part of the world economy. Really! You and your family are involved in world trade every day. The proof is in your closets and garage. Look around your house to see if you can find items that were made in other countries.

1. Search your closet and dresser. Read the labels on your clothes. Where were your clothes made?
2. Examine your kitchen cupboard and refrigerator. Look for labels on cans and packages. Where was the food grown or packaged?
3. Check out your family's garage, driveway, or parking lot. Find the names of the automobiles. Where were they made?

Making a Living Today

When Connecticut went from being a colony to being a state, most people farmed. Farming is still very important in our state. But today most people work in service jobs. They are engineers, drivers, and teachers. Many people also work in manufacturing or retail jobs.

(Photo by John Ivanko)

Agriculture

Farmers grow crops and *livestock*. Livestock means animals raised to make money by selling their meat, eggs, or milk.

Farmers sell eggs and chickens to nearby cities. Dairy farming is also important. Most of Connecticut's dairy farmers produce milk to sell. They also raise cattle, sheep, and hogs.

Hay, sweet corn, and tobacco are our state's main crops. Connecticut Shadegrown is a kind of tobacco used for cigar wrappers. You can see tobacco barns and fields along some of our highways. Connecticut farmers sell corn to local stores and at stands along the sides of country roads. Apples are our main fruit crop.

Manufacturing

Manufacturing goods has been an important way to make a living since colonial times.

Today, Connecticut companies make computers, office machines, helicopters, aircraft engines, propellers, ships, submarines, hand tools, and knives. They produce chemicals, medicines, and soaps. They make high-tech instruments for surgery.

Some Connecticut Manufacturers

COMPANY	PRODUCT	CITY
Pitney Bowes Inc.	Postage meters	Stamford
The Stanley Works	Tools, hardware	New Britain
Electric Boat Shipyard	Submarines, ships	Groton
United Technologies	Aircraft, helicopters	Hartford
Bic Corporation	Pens, pencils	Milford

Service Industries

People in service industries do not raise crops or manufacture goods. Instead, they do something to help people. Doctors, lawyers, teachers, nurses, and sales people work in service industries. Government workers also provide many services.

Banks, insurance companies, and real estate firms also serve people. They help people with their money and property. Insurance has been a big business in Hartford for many years.

Tourism

When people visit Connecticut, they may eat at Frank Pepe's Pizzeria in New Haven or visit the Wadsworth Atheneum in Hartford. They might go to Hammonasset Beach State Park in Madison, or cheer at a Brigdeport Bluefish game. This is all part of *tourism*—a major industry in Connecticut.

Tourists love to visit the seal pool at the Norwalk Maritime Museum.
(Photo by Scott Barrow)

Tourism provides jobs and money because people come to Connecticut and spend money on transportation, lodging, food, entertainment, and recreation. All of the things tourists do in our state make money for the businesses and workers of Connecticut.

Ekaterina Gordeeva has trained at the International Skating Center of Connecticut.

Simsbury

Ice Skating Capital of the World!

Whether you like to skate on a frozen pond or in a high-tech rink, Connecticut is the place to do it! Some of the world's best figure skaters train at the International Skating Center of Connecticut in Simsbury. They come and stay for months at a time. Some of them live here so they can be close to the ice rink and coaches all year round. Tourists come to watch them perform.

The Connecticut Adventure

Non-Profit Organizations

A *non-profit* organization hires people to make the world a better place. The employees get paid, but the organization does not make a profit. Any money it makes goes to programs that help people.

Here are a few non-profit groups in Connecticut:

Some Connecticut Non-Profit Organizations

NAME	PLACE	JOB
Habitat for Humanity	Northeast Connecticut	Builds houses for poor families
Connecticut Maritime Association	Stamford	Helps people who work in the shipping industry
Heart to Heart Community Services/Food Pantry	Norwich	Helps feed poor people
Neighbors and Newcomers	New Milford	Helps welcome people and build new friendships

What do you think?

Someday you will be a grownup. If you could choose any job in the world, what would it be?

What part of the economy would your job be in: farming, manufacturing, or service? Would it be at a non-profit company?

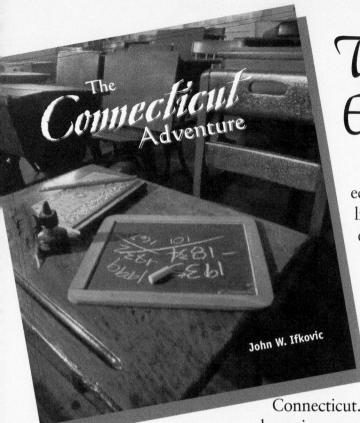

The
Connecticut
Adventure

John W. Ifkovic

The Connecticut Economic Adventure!

This book is a good example of how free-enterprise economics works. An entrepreneur started a book publishing company. The owner of the company and his employees decided that they wanted to make a book that children would really like. They also hoped the teachers would like the book enough to buy it, so the company would make a profit. It took the services and products of many people in different parts of the world to make this book. Here is what happened:

The author in Connecticut studied Connecticut history. He went to libraries and read books about Connecticut. He read the diaries of people who had lived here a long time ago. He typed the words on a computer. He worked hard to make the book interesting and tell a true story of Connecticut.

The editor in Massachusetts was in charge of making sure the spelling and writing were right. She found the photographs. An artist in Utah drew some of the pictures. A different artist used a computer to arrange the words and pictures on each page. All of these things took over a year to do.

When the book was ready to be printed, it was sent across the Pacific Ocean to China. The paper came from trees in Asia. Someone made and sold the ink to the printer. Many workers there printed the book on huge presses. They used machines to sew the pages together and glue the covers on. After about four months, the books were brought to America on a ship. The ship landed in California. Then large boxes of books were brought to Connecticut in trucks.

All of the people who worked on the book had to be paid for their services. All of the machines,

238

computers, paper, and even ink had to be paid for. Where did the money come from?

You and your friends are the consumers. Your school paid for your books. The schools got the money from the government. The government got the money from taxes. The taxes were paid by the adults in your town. The people earned the money to pay their taxes from their jobs or businesses.

So there you have it! People work hard to provide the goods and services other people need. The work makes them feel good about themselves. It provides money for the workers and their families. The work helps provide for the needs of everyone.

Making a book is an adventure! It is part of the economics of Connecticut and other places in the world.

Making a Living in Connecticut

Goods or Services

Goods are things that are usually manufactured. This means they are made in factories, workshops, or even at home. They are then sold for money. Shoes, pencils, televisions, and dog collars are all goods. People make money by making and selling goods.

Services are things that people do for other people. Dentists, sales clerks, umpires, coaches, and your teacher are providing services. People earn money by providing services.

On a separate piece of paper, number from one to twelve. Write "G" next to the jobs that produce goods and "S" next to the jobs that perform services.

1. Fixes the plumbing
2. Collects the garbage
3. Teaches students
4. Manufactures paint
5. Makes engines for cars
6. Repairs cars
7. Delivers cheese to grocery stores
8. Makes telephones
9. Repairs telephones
10. Manufactures light bulbs
11. Sells light bulbs
12. _____ (What you would like to do when you grow up)

Activity

My Community

• What goods are made in your community? Look around your city or town. Look in the phone book. On a separate piece of paper, list five goods made right in your community.

• Write two paragraphs describing how your city or town has changed over time. Do people make a living the same way they did fifty or a hundred years ago? What are some of the newest businesses in your community?

Chapter 13 Review

1. If you work for someone else, you are an _____.

2. How do Connecticut businesses make a profit?

3. What is supply and demand?

4. What is an entrepreneur?

5. What are the four factors of production?

6. Name one Connecticut entrepreneur and the product he or she makes.

7. List two types of transportation and why each is important to Connecticut's businesses.

8. What are two industries in Connecticut today?

9. What are two crops grown in Connecticut today?

10. List at least three jobs that provide services. Tell why they are services, not goods.

11. How do tourists help make money for Connecticut?

12. What is a non-profit organization?

Geography Tie-In

Have a brainstorming session with your classmates about how geography affects businesses. Choose a business that you know of. Then describe how it is affected by the land (is it flat or hilly, on the coast or inland?). Discuss what transportation, natural resources, and workers the business uses. Talk about how the business might affect the environment.

Glossary

The meanings of these words are according to their use in the chapters of this textbook.

Forms of speech are abbreviated.
(adj) = adjective (describes a noun)
(n) = noun (a person, place, or thing)
(v) = verb (an action word)

abolitionist: *(n)* a person who fought to end slavery

aerospace: *(adj)* having to do with air and space

ally: *(n)* a country that helps another country protect itself

ambassador: *(n)* someone sent to another country to represent our government

amendment: *(n)* a change or addition to make something better

ammunition: *(n)* bullets and other military explosives

apprentice: *(n)* a person who lives with a craftsman and learns a trade

arsenal: *(n)* a place where guns and weapons are made or stored

artifact: *(n)* an object left behind by people long ago

assassinate: *(v)* to murder by sudden attack

astronomy: *(n)* the study of the planets and stars

atlatl: *(n)* a tool that helped early people throw a spear

atomic: *(adj)* having to do with nuclear energy

auction: *(n)* a sale where whoever bids the most money gets the item

bayonet: *(n)* a spear that fits on the end of a rifle

bill: *(n)* a written idea for a law

blacksmith: *(n)* a person who shapes iron into tools and other items such as horseshoes

border state: *(n)* in Civil War times, a state located between the northern and southern states

boycott: *(v)* to stop buying something in order to make a point

canal: *(n)* a waterway made by people, not nature

candidate: *(n)* a person who tries to get elected to office

capitalistic: *(adj)* having an economic system in which the people, not the government, own and run businesses and businesses compete with each other

casino: *(n)* a building where gamblers make bets and play cards

century: *(n)* a period of 100 years

charter: *(n)* a paper that gives permission to settle a piece of land

civil rights: *(n)* the rights that belong to every citizen

civil war: *(n)* a war between people of the same country

climate: *(n)* the weather of an area over a long period of time

concentration camp: *(n)* a horrible prison camp for Germany's prisoners during World War II

Confederacy: *(n)* the group of southern states that tried to form their own country during the Civil War

conquer: *(v)* to take over by force

communism: *(n)* a system in which the government, not the people, owns and runs the businesses

commuter: *(adj)* having to do with people getting to work and back

compromise: *(n)* an agreement reached where each side gives up part of its demands

congregation: *(n)* a group of people of the same religion who meet together

consumer: *(n)* a person who spends money on goods or services

corrupt: *(adj)* evil or rotten

council: *(n)* a group of people who meet to talk about something important

covenant: *(n)* an official agreement between two or more people

culture: *(n)* a way of life

debt: *(n)* money owed

defense: *(n)* the protection of a country

degree: *(n)* a unit of measurement for part of a circle or globe

delegate: *(n)* someone chosen to speak or act for a group of people

democracy: *(n)* government by the people

depression: *(n)* a time when there are very few jobs and people are very poor

dictator: *(n)* a ruler with all the power

discipline: *(n)* control; following the rules

discrimination: *(n)* treating people unfairly just because they are different

district: *(n)* a part of a larger place

economics: *(n)* the study of how people use their resources to make, sell, buy, and use goods and services

economy: *(n)* the way people use their resources to make, sell, buy, and use goods and services

ecosystem: *(n)* a community of living things that interact and depend upon each other

elect: *(v)* to choose by vote

emissions: *(n)* particles put into the air

empire: *(n)* a group of countries or territories that are controlled by one government

employee: *(n)* a person who works for wages

entrepreneur: *(n)* a person who has an idea and the courage to start a business

equator: *(n)* an imaginary line around the middle of the earth

ethnic group: *(n)* a group of people of the same culture or race

evaporate: *(v)* to turn liquid into vapor or air

expense: *(n)* a cost; money spent

extinct: *(n)* no longer existing on earth

fertile: *(adj)* allowing lots of things to grow well

fertilize: *(v)* to add material to the soil so crops will grow better

flax: *(n)* a plant fiber used to make cloth

fleet: *(n)* a group of warships

free enterprise: *(adj)* having the freedom to do what a business wants without the government getting too involved

frontier: *(n)* the edge of settled territory

generator: *(n)* a machine that makes electricity

geography: *(n)* the study of the earth and the people, animals, and plants living on it

glacier: *(n)* a large mass of ice built up over a long time

good: *(n)* a product that is made, bought, and sold

grant: *(n)* permission to settle on a piece of land

graze: *(v)* to feed on grass or pasture

gristmill: *(n)* a mill for grinding grain into flour

growing season: *(n)* the time between the last frost of spring and the first frost of fall; the time when farmers can grow crops

harbor: *(n)* a sheltered part of a body of water

deep enough for anchoring ships

heroine: *(n)* a woman admired for her achievements and character; a female hero

Holocaust: *(n)* the killing of European Jews and others in Nazi concentration camps during World War II

House of Representatives: *(n)* one of the two houses of Congress, made up of representatives from the fifty states

humid: *(adj)* damp; moist

idle: *(adj)* having nothing to do; wasting time

immigrant: *(n)* a person who moves to a new country to live

income tax: *(n)* a tax on the money a person earns

independence: *(n)* freedom from another country's control

independent: *(adj)* not ruled by anyone else; acting on your own

Industrial Revolution: *(n)* a change from producing things by hand to using machines

influence: *(v)* to affect people or make them change their minds

insurance: *(n)* a policy that says that a company will pay the cost if something bad happens

interchangeable: *(adj)* able to change places with something else

interstate: *(n)* a highway that goes through several states

ironworks: *(n)* a mill or factory in which iron or steel is made

jury: *(n)* a group of people who listen to a case and decide if a person is innocent or guilty of breaking the law

labor union: *(n)* a group of workers who get

together to cause change

latitude: *(n)* imaginary lines that measure how far north or south of the equator a place is

legislator: *(n)* a person elected to make the laws

livestock: *(n)* farm animals that are sold or used for profit

local government: *(n)* government that is close to home, such as town or city government

longitude: *(n)* imaginary lines that measure how far east or west of the prime meridian a place is

loom: *(n)* a machine that weaves thread or yarn together to make cloth

loyalist: *(n)* a person in the thirteen colonies who was loyal to the king of England

majority: *(n)* more than half of the people

massacre: *(n)* the violent killing of a lot of people

mass production: *(n)* making many things at once, usually with machines

merchant: *(n)* someone who buys and sells things or runs a store

middle-class: *(adj)* not rich or poor but in the middle

militia: *(n)* a small local army

monarchy: *(n)* government by one ruler, such as a king or queen

mutiny: *(n)* a revolt against the captain of a ship

natural resource: *(n)* something found in nature that people use

nominate: *(v)* to name or choose as a candidate

non-profit: *(adj)* not done to make money

nourish: *(v)* to feed with healthy things

nuclear: *(adj)* having to do with atomic energy or bombs

ordinance: *(n)* a local law

overseer: *(n)* a person who has the job of watching others to make sure they work

patriot: *(n)* a person who wanted the thirteen colonies to be free of the rule of England; someone who loves his or her country

pattern of settlement: *(n)* the way people settle

peddler: *(n)* someone who sells things door to door or town to town

pelt: *(n)* the skin of a furry animal

permanent: *(adj)* lasting a long time

pillory: *(n)* a wooden frame with locks in which a person's head and hands were placed for punishment

plantation: *(n)* a large farming estate

point of view: *(n)* the way someone views something

political party: *(n)* an organized group of people who share the same ideas about government

politics: *(n)* the activities of government

powwow: *(n)* a Native American meeting or celebration

prejudice: *(n)* an opinion made before the facts are known; a judgment made about a person just on the basis of race or religion

preserve: *(v)* to keep something in its natural condition

privateer: *(n)* a sailor who has permission to attack enemy ships

profit: *(n)* the money left after expenses are paid

Progressive: *(n)* a person who wanted the government to solve social problems

prohibit: *(v)* to forbid

protest: *(v)* to complain against an idea or action; to speak out against something

proverb: *(n)* a saying that has a lesson in it

provision: *(n)* a stock of supplies

purify: *(v)* to make pure

Puritan: *(n)* a member of a religious group that believed in simple churches and ceremonies and thought the Church of England was corrupt

ratify: *(v)* to sign something to show you agree

ration: *(n)* a little bit of something divided among many people

raw materials: *(n)* materials used to make something else

rebellion: *(n)* a fight against those in power

reform: *(v)* to change for the better

refuge: *(n)* a place set apart to protect animals and plants

region: *(n)* an area that has things in common, such as landforms or economic activity

reliable: *(adj)* able to be depended on

renaissance: *(n)* a rebirth or new beginning

representative: *(n)* someone elected to speak or act for others

representative democracy: *(n)* a type of government in which the people choose representatives to vote and make the laws for them

republic: *(n)* a government in which the people have the power to vote and where there is usually a president

reservation: *(n)* land set aside by the government for Native Americans

revive: *(v)* to wake up or bring back to life

revolution: *(n)* when one government takes over another government

ritual: (n) religious customs or ceremonies

rural: (adj) having to do with the country (not the city)

sachem: (n) a Native American chief or leader

salary: (n) money paid to an employee on a regular basis

sea level: (n) the level of the ocean where it meets the land

secede: (v) to break off from a country

segregation: (n) separation by race

selectmen: (n) people who are elected to run a town

Senate: (n) one of the two houses in Congress, made up of two representatives from each state

service: (n) in economics, something done for another person for money

sinew: (n) a tendon or tissue from inside an animal

slave: (n) a person who is owned by another person and forced to work for someone else without pay

sound: (n) a narrow stretch of water between larger bodies of water or between the mainland and an island

steerage: (n) the lower part of a ship where passengers who paid the lowest fare stayed

stock: (n) money invested in business

strike: (n) a protest where workers stop work until a change or agreement is made

suburb: (n) an area with houses and streets just outside of a city

suffrage: (n) the right to vote

supply and demand: (n) a rule in economics; how much there is of something affects how much it will cost

symbol: (n) something that stands for something else

tax: (v) to make the people pay money to the government

tenement: (n) a low-rent apartment building

textile: (n) woven or knit cloth

toll: (n) money paid for using a road

tourism: (n) when people take a vacation in another place

town green: (n) an open area in the center of a town, usually planted with grass

traitor: (n) a person who turns against his friends and joins the enemy; someone who betrays trust

tributary: (n) a small river that flows into a larger river or body of water

tundra: (n) a large open stretch of frozen land

Underground Railroad: (n) a secret system of routes that slaves used to escape to freedom

Union: (n) the northern states during the Civil War

communism: (n) a system in which the government, not the people, owns and runs the businesses

vehicle: (n) a car, truck, tank; something that carries something else

veto: (n) a power of the president or governor to stop a bill from becoming a law

wage: (n) money paid to workers

wampum: (n) Native American beadwork made from tiny shells

Index

Credits

DRAWINGS
Burton, Jon 69, 102-103, 132, 230-231

Cornia, Ray 65

Litterer, Marie (Courtesy of the Pratt Museum at Amherst College) Contents page (second from top left), 24-25

Rasmussen, Gary vii, 11, 14, 15, 19, 20, 24 (bottom), 26, 27, 32 (top), 36, 37, 38, 39, 43, 49, 78, 84, 95 (bottom left), 99, 107, 125, 169 (both), 183 (top right), 225

Wilbur, C. Keith (from *The New England Indians* with permission from the Globe-Pequot Press) 25 (bottom left), 31, 32 (bottom), 33, 34 (left margin, top and bottom)

MAPS
by Richard Elton

PAINTINGS
Henry, Carl (Courtesy of the Prudence Crandall House) 126

PHOTOGRAPHS
Amherst History Museum 60 (top left) 76 (bottom), 82

Archive Photos 41 (bottom left), 50, 53, 87, 88, 89, 90 (top), 97 (top, center, and bottom right) 98, 112, (top left), 113, 136

Barrow, Scott Contents page (second from bottom right), 7 (both), 10 (top center), 13 (bottom right), 17 (left), 203, 208-209, 232, 236 (top)

Blanchette, David 28

Bluh, Geoffrey 197

Chamberlain, Lynn 15 (top left)

Cincinnati Historical Society 131 (bottom left), 138 (top)

Clineff, Kindra Contents page (third from bottom right, bottom right), 8, 9 (top right), 10-11 (background, bottom left), 13 (top), 14, 16 (both), 17 (right), 19, 62 (center), 117 (top right), 154 (inset), 157 (bottom), 192-193, 210,

Colonial Williamsburg 67

Connecticut Historical Society 41 (bottom right), 45, 47, 52 (bottom left), 54 (both), 56 (bottom), 60 (bottom), 62 (left), 68, 104 (top left), 109 (bottom right detail), 115 (both), 117 (bottom right), 130 (bottom left), 136 (right), 149, 152 (bottom left), 154, 157 (top), 161 (top), 164 (bottom left), 165 (both), 176 (bottom center), 184, 201 (top right)

Crossman, Jean (Courtesy of the Amherst History Museum) 60 (top left), 76 (bottom), 82

Demarchelier, Patrick (Courtesy of Martha Stewart Living Omnimedia Inc. All rights reserved.) 228 (top left)

Evans, Middleton 195

George Eastman House 53 (bottom), 159, 162 (center), 168 (top left)

Greater Toledo Convention & Visitors' Bureau 64 (bottom left)

Halloran, Bob (Courtesy of the Mashantucket Pequot Museum) 35, 38

Hartford Courant 198 (top left)

Hartford Public Library 200 (top left)

History of Maryland Slide Collection (Instructional Resources Corporation) Contents page (top right)

Illinois Historical Society 175 (left), 181 (top right)

Index Stock Imagery 194

International Skating Center of Connecticut 236 (bottom center and left)

Ivanko, John 118, 234 (center)

Joshua Hempsted House, Antiquarian & Landmarks Society 141 (top)

Lange, Dorothea 181 (bottom)

Library of Congress 130-131, 161 (bottom right), 185 (top right), 202 (top left), 213 (top right)

Lynn, John 15 (bottom)

Martha Stewart Living Omnimedia, Inc. All rights reserved. 228 (top left)

Mashantucket Pequot Museum and Research Center 30, 35, 38

McConnell, Jack (McConnell & McNamara) Contents page (middle left), 52 (top left), 58-59, 65 (bottom right), 124, 167 (both)

McCullagh, Declan 204 (top left)

Michigan State Archives 168 (bottom center)

New Haven Colony Historical Society 51, 137

New Jersey Newsphotos 199 (bottom

Newman's Own, Inc. 229 (bottom left

North Wind Picture Archives Content page (third from top left, third from bottom left, second from bottom left, bottom left), 40-41, 46, 56 (top left), 58 (bottom), 59 (bottom), 63 (bottom), 64 (bottom center), 72, 77-78, 83, 94-95, 108-109, 108 (bottom), 114, 116, 120, 122, 133 140, 144

Office of John C. Rowland 212

Office of Joseph Lieberman 214

Office of Rosa DeLauro 214 (center)

Peale Museum, Baltimore 162 (left)

Phillips, Allen (Courtesy of the Mashantucket Pequot Museum) 3

Prudence Crandall Museum 126, 127

Rogers, Lillie 228 (bottom)

Shutterstock.com 2-3, 157, 192-193, 210, 220-221

Sikorsky Aircraft Company 196

Smithsonian Museum 73

Subway Restaurants 229 (top right)

Till, Tom Contents page (top left), 9 (bottom), 12, 139 (bottom)

Toledo Convention and Visitors Burea 64 (bottom left)

Trumbull Historical Society Photo Collection 90 (bottom)

Union Pacific Railroad Museum Collection 119

University of Oregon Library Content page (second from top right), 152-153

U.S. Navy, Submarine Force Museum 91 (both)

Utah State Historical Society 122, 18 (bottom), 227

Yale University Library 73 (bottom)

All photographs not listed are from the collection of Gibbs Smith, Publisher.